PUNCTUATION

CARL MARKGRAF, Ph.D.
Portland State University

under the auspices of
Portland State University,
Division of Continuing Education

John Wiley & Sons, Inc., Publishers

New York • Chichester • Brisbane • Toronto

Editor: Judy Wilson
Production Manager: Ken Burke
Editorial Supervisor: Ken Burke
Page Make-up: Meredythe

Library of Congress Cataloging in Publication Data:

Markgraf, Carl.
    Punctuation.

    (Wiley self-teaching guides)
    Includes index.
    1. English language—Punctuation.
2. English language—Self-instruction.   I. Title.
PE1450.M337   428'.2   79-18613
ISBN 0-471-03100-3

Printed in the United States of America

79 80 10 9 8 7 6 5 4 3 2 1

Acknowledgments

My thanks go to the unsung authors of the original *Punctuation* for many of the insights I gained from their work in the self-teaching format and to Professor Alex Scharbach for his advice to undertake the project. My thanks also to the English Department of Portland State University for support in manuscript preparation, and especially to Diane Smith.

Public thanks to my wife, Barbara, for her forthright criticism and patient reading of more first drafts than any woman ought to expect from a set of marriage vows—this is long overdue.

Preface

Punctuation first appeared under the auspices of the Teaching Research Division of the Oregon State System of Higher Education. A cooperative venture that utilized the teaching talents and experience of scores of college writing teachers, *Punctuation* was one of a series of "programmed learning" texts sponsored by the Commission. In that form, over the years it served thousands of writing students whose college instructors recommended its use in improving their basic skills.

This new version of *Punctuation* retains the thoroughly tested logic and organization of the original. At the same time, it both expands the coverage of punctuation problems and provides greater opportunity for a "hands-on" experience through numerous practice sections. Since the original book was intended for school use, its writers could rely on the student's access to a teacher for answers to unforeseen problems and for more examples if needed. This book is designed to provide the needed materials, and to supply the answers to possible questions, independent of other help.

Punctuation does not, however, cover everything there is to be learned about the subject. Every specialized field of writing—scientific, literary, musical, business—has its own individual tricks of the trade. Many business firms have a few punctuation peculiarities they expect their writers to follow. Obviously, no book can cover all these variations on standard punctuation. But what *can* be covered—and what this book does cover—are the basic punctuation skills on which these special uses are built. These skills are largely a matter of common sense, not memorization of rules, and can be easily learned through practice. After all, punctuation marks are only the signposts we all use in finding our way through the written word to the meaning behind it. Meaningful use of punctuation is the whole point of this book.

Portland, Oregon
April, 1979

Carl Markgraf

To the Reader

How you punctuate can make a big difference in whether or not you communicate the meaning you intended. *Punctuation* is designed to teach you how to use punctuation most effectively to enhance the meaning of what you write. As with other Wiley Self-Teaching Guides, its approach is practical rather than theoretical, stressing areas of greatest importance to you in business, office, or personal use.

Punctuation is a self-instructional book designed so you can learn at your own pace and study only what interests you. As you begin each chapter, look at the list of objectives. These objectives outline what you can expect to learn from each chapter. If the material is already familiar to you, take the Self-Test at the end of the chapter. If you do well, you can skip the chapter without reading it. If you miss some questions, you should review the parts of the chapter indicated in parentheses after the Self-Test answers. In this way you read only the material you need, without wasting time on material you already know.

Throughout the book you will be applying each new concept or skill as you learn it. Each chapter is divided into numbered steps called frames. Each frame gives you some information and then asks you to write an answer or to choose between alternative answers. You will be able to check the accuracy of your answers by immediately comparing them with the correct response which appears below the dashed line. (You may wish to cover the answer with a card or a piece of paper until you've answered the question.) Be sure you understand the material before you go to the next frame.

At the end of each chapter is a Self-Test containing a good cross-section of problems similar to the ones you solved in the chapter. If you have trouble with any of these problems, you can review the frames indicated in parentheses following their solution. At the end of *Punctuation* is a Final Test covering the whole book, complete with chapter and frame references for review.

Contents

CHAPTER ONE

The Need for Punctuation

Punctuation is simple and necessary.

Some people may agree with the second adjective in that sentence, admitting grudgingly that punctuation is "necessary"; but many may dispute that first adjective, "simple." They remember all the punctuation drills they underwent during their school years in an attempt to learn the "rules" of punctuation, and they recall their frustration in discovering that there were usually as many exceptions as there were rules.

Yet punctuation *is* simpler than many people suspect. It is not really a mass of meaningless rules, arbitrarily imposed by some authority; it is almost entirely a matter of simple logic and common sense. Far from being something that is "stuck onto" writing like a useless decoration, it is actually very closely related to the *meaning* of what we write.

Briefly, then, the purposes of this first chapter on punctuation are: to illustrate some of the main functions of English punctuation, to show its necessity, and to begin improving your accuracy in using it for your own needs.

OBJECTIVES

When you have completed this chapter, you should be able to:

- use punctuation to alter the meaning of a sentence;
- use punctuation to make sense out of a sentence;
- use the period, question mark, and exclamation point to indicate intonation and stress.

THE NEED FOR PUNCTUATION

1.　Let's demonstrate first the necessity for punctuation. To see how much you rely on it, try reading the following group of letters. After you have done so, supply the punctuation that would make the job easier.

　　ihittheballwiththebat

_ _ _ _ _ _ _ _ _ _ _ _ _ _ _

I hit the ball with the bat.

　　What did you have to do to the sentence? Not much, really. You capitalized the first letter and put a period at the end; and of course you separated the words by spacing between them. Space itself is a form of "punctuation," since it shows how you want a series of letters to be grouped and what words you want those letters to form. In this same way, other punctuation marks—commas, periods, semicolons, for instance—show what words you want to group together to form a phrase or thought, or to make a single statement. So the slight changes you made in punctuating the sample sentence had a great deal to do with making it easier to read.

For another example, see how this last paragraph looks without punctuation marks.

　　What did you have to do to the above sentence not much really you capitalized the first letter and put a period at the end and of course you separated the words by spacing between them space itself is a form of punctuation since it shows how you want a series of letters to be grouped and what words you want those letters to form in this same way other punctuation marks commas periods semicolons for instance show what words you want to group together to form a phrase or thought or to make a single statement the slight changes you made in punctuating the sample sentence had a great deal to do with making it easier to read for another example see how this paragraph looks without punctuation marks

　　When punctuation is missing, it's easy to see that it's there not to distract you, but to guide you, to help you follow the writer's thought.

2.　So too in your own writing, the most important principle to recognize in using punctuation is that it is not a mere ornament or distraction; it is an absolute necessity, directly connected with the meaning of what you write. Let's sum up this basic principle: The best argument in favor of using punctuation accurately is that it is closely related to the

_____ of your writing.

— — — — — — — — — — — — — — — —

meaning. That's right!

3.   In case you're still not convinced, let's look at a few more examples.
      These will show again that meaningful punctuation is not so much a
      matter of memorizing and following certain "rules," as of applying
      ordinary reasoning to make the meaning clear.
          Punctuate the following sentence:

      Before entering college at the age of eighteen Henry travelled widely.

— — — — — — — — — — — — — — — —

      The sentence makes sense if it is punctuated in either of these ways:

      (a)   Before entering college, at the age of eighteen Henry travelled
             widely.
      (b)   Before entering college at the age of eighteen, Henry travelled
             widely.

      (Note that if you used *two* commas, before and after the phrase "at the
      age of eighteen," you haven't really solved the problem. You have sort
      of retired the phrase without showing which part of the sentence it
      should be linked to, so it just "floats" there without giving meaning.)

4.   What's the problem in the sentence in frame 3? It is to determine what
      it was that Henry did at the age of eighteen. Does the sentence mean
      he entered college, or does it mean he travelled widely? Logically, he
      could have done either one; so the phrase "at the age of eighteen" could
      be linked to either part of the sentence and make perfectly good sense.
      Without any punctuation to guide the reader, the sentence has two
      equally but quite different meanings. What are they? Rewrite the above
      two sentences so as to emphasize their different meanings.

      (a)

      (b)

— — — — — — — — — — — — — — — —

Two possible versions are:

(a)   When Henry was eighteen, he travelled widely; and some time later—when he was nineteen, perhaps, or twenty, or thirty, or sixty-five—he entered college.
(b)   When Henry was eighteen, he entered college; and some time before that—when he was two, perhaps, or twelve, or seventeen—he travelled widely.

Again notice that both sentences, as punctuated in frame 3, make perfectly good sense—but that the meaning is changed entirely by the simple placement of a comma. There is no "rule" to follow here. The example merely shows how *you*, as a writer, must use punctuation intelligently to make your writing communicate the meaning *you* want it to have.

5.   Now let's try another similar sentence, in which once again the placement of the punctuation will determine the meaning. Punctuate this group of words in two different ways, leading to different but equally logical meanings.

As we watched the coach a heavy-set man approached us.

(a)

(b)

— — — — — — — — — — — — — — — —

(a)   As we watched, the coach, a heavy-set man, approached us.
(b)   As we watched the coach, a heavy-set man approached us.

Let's see what our punctuation has done to the meaning. In the first version, "we" are watching something—a football game or some other athletic contest. As we watch, the coach approaches us, and we see that he is a heavy-set man. In the second version, "we" are watching the coach; and while we watch him, someone else, who happens to be a heavy-set man, approaches us.

Yes, both sentences make sense, and they could easily occur in your writing. But there are obvious differences in meaning, not the least of which is the fact that in the first sentence the "coach" and the "heavy-set man" are one and the same person, whereas in the second sentence they are two entirely different persons. What about a "rule"?

Again, there is none. The writer alone knows the exact intended meaning, and he or she must use the punctuation that will express exactly that meaning, and no other.

6. Even when only one meaning seems possible, some ingenious people can find others. How would you punctuate this sentence? Try for more than one version.

    Dick doesnt know what time it is but hell ask

Dick doesn't know what time it is, but he'll ask.

This is one answer, and it's probably the way you punctuated it. (The comma after "is" may be optional, since the clauses are very short, but it does indicate a slight vocal hesitation between the two statements.) But you also might have punctuated the sentence this way:

Dick doesn't know what time it is, but hell, ask!

Right? Yes, of course. The sentence makes perfectly good sense that way—and that, after all, is what punctuation is supposed to do, isn't it? In the second version the tone of the sentence has changed a good deal, but that's only further proof of the importance of punctuation and its close relationship to the meaning of what you write.

7. One more illustration. The sentences we just used as illustrations are perfectly ordinary ones that could occur in your own writing. But there are many trick sentences—at least they seem like trick sentences without their punctuation. Unpunctuated, they are totally meaningless groups of words which, surprisingly, become meaningful when the appropriate punctuation is added. Try this one. Nothing needs to be changed, and nothing needs to be added, except some punctuation.

    that that is is that that is not is not is that it it is

That that is, is. That that is not, is not. Is that it? It is!

Notice something new that punctuation is doing in this example. Not only is it sorting out the meaning of an otherwise meaningless collection of words, it's adding two other functions: first, the question mark gives a "lift" to the mental voice as we read it, an intonation we all recognize as the oral signal for a question; and second, the exclamation mark adds its own kind of "punch" to the statement, almost as if we were shouting the words "It is!" So, punctuation also helps to communicate our feelings about what we're saying.

Before going on to the functions and uses of the basic punctuation marks, let's re-examine what we've discovered so far.

SELF-TEST

This Self-Test will help you determine how well you have met the objectives of this chapter and whether you are ready to go on to the next chapter. The answers to this Self-Test follow.

1. Punctuation is not a rigid system of arbitrary rules; it is a series of marks designed to help us group and arrange our thoughts. Punctuation relates

    closely and inherently to the ____meaning____ of what you write.

2. You can change the meaning of a sentence by changing its punctuation. Punctuate the following sentence in two ways so that it has different meanings:

    Before we beached the canoe at noon we ate our lunch.

    (a)

    (b)

3. Punctuate the following so it makes sense:

    everything that is is good this is is it good youd better believe it

Answers to Self-Test

Compare your answer to the Self-Test with those given below. If you answered all questions correctly, go on to the next chapter. If you missed any, review the frames indicated in parentheses following the answers. If you missed several questions, you should probably look back over the whole chapter before going on.

1. meaning (frame 2)

2. (a) Before we beached the canoe at noon, we ate our lunch.
    (b) Before we beached the canoe, at noon we ate our lunch.
    (frames 3, 4, 5)
    (When did we beach the canoe? When did we eat our lunch? Depends on the comma.)

3. Everything that is, is good. This is. Is it good? You'd better believe it!
    (frame 6)

CHAPTER TWO

Whole Sentence Punctuation

In this chapter we will cover how to punctuate the whole sentence. Let's begin with the whole sentence. A group of words making up a complete sentence customarily ends with one of three different punctuation marks. The mark itself tells our eye that a statement has been completed. Furthermore, it indicates what kind of statement it has been—declarative, interrogative, or exclamatory—three terms that almost explain themselves. A declarative sentence declares something, makes a declaration, states a fact: "The customs man found the extra cigarettes I hid in my luggage." (Well, I declare! Rather, I should have declared!) An interrogative sentence asks a direct question, makes an interrogation: "Where were you on the night in question, Mark?" And an exclamatory sentence makes a statement that is genuinely emphatic: "We're on fire! Abandon ship!" As we saw with the sentences in the last chapter, the choice of punctuation you make will affect the meaning of the sentences you write. The same sentence with different ending punctuation will be quite different. For example:

    (a)   He lost the ball on the two-yard line.
    (b)   He lost the ball on the two-yard line?
    (c)   He lost the ball on the two-yard line!

Notice this about the last two sentences: *how* they are understood depends on how the reader or writer feels about them; the writer's intentions are involved. In (b) and (c) the writer might have added: "How awful!" if his own team were involved, or "How terrific!" if the opposition lost the ball. But whether or not the writer's intentions are clear, as here they are not because we lack sufficient information, it is obvious that a different punctuation mark makes a great difference in the sentences' meanings.

OBJECTIVES

When you have completed this chapter, you should be able to:

- identify declarative, interrogative, and exclamatory sentences;
- apply meaningful end punctuation to these sentence types.

1. So far we've not *named* the three marks of punctuation that may end a sentence. Did you notice? Look back now at the three examples about our slippery-fingered ball-player in the introduction above, and list the names of the three types of end punctuation:

    (a) _____

    (b) _____

    (c) _____

    _____

    (a) periods; (b) question marks; (c) exclamation points;

    All these symbols show that a thought has been stated completely, and they also tell the reader something about the pitch or stress to be given the words "in the mind's ear."

2. Punctuation marks are thus intimately related to sentence structure: they mark a word or phrase that can stand alone (*Well? Don't they? Yes, of course. That's obvious!*—these are all examples), or a whole sentence. And they serve as well to clarify the meaning and to establish the emphasis of the sentences whose boundaries they mark.

    As we saw above, the period follows the declarative sentence, the question mark follows the interrogative sentence, and the exclamation point follows the strongly emphatic sentence. Look at this sentence:

    The freight you inquired about in your last letter was shipped from our Oakland plant on June 4, 1923.

    Check one:

    ____ (a) It asks a question.

    ____ (b) It makes a statement.

    ____ (c) It indicates strong emotion.

    _____

    (b) It makes a statement.

3.   Since the sentence makes a statement, it should be followed by

_____ (a)   an exclamation point

_____ (b)   a question mark

_____ (c)   a period

- - - - - - - - - - - - - - -

(c)   a period

4.   Not only does a period follow all sentences that make a statement, including indirect questions, but also it marks the end of mildly imperative sentences as well. For example: "He asked if I felt well." is an indirect question. "Put the box down." is a mild command. Both use periods. Try this one:

> Peterson asked the doctors to allow him to see her once more before he left

This sentence should be followed by _____ .

- - - - - - - - - - - - - - -

a period. The sentence is an indirect question.

5.   Now try this:

> Yes, please, set the chest there by the door

This sentence should be followed by _____ .

- - - - - - - - - - - - - - -

a period. The sentence is not emphatic; it's a mild command.

6.   Here's another:

> My God An avalanche Look out Stand back

The parts of this example could be followed by _____ .

- - - - - - - - - - - - - - -

exclamation points

7.   Broken exclamations involving strong emotion and giving strong or urgent commands make use of one or more exclamation points. The

exclamation point is not often used in formal business writing, except where it may appear in order to arouse interest. In a "sales pitch," for example, we often see "Buy now!" "Don't miss this opportunity!" "Here's your chance to save big bucks!" But the exclamation point often does appear in our personal correspondence, where we want to share our strong feelings with friends. Even in such writing, however, we need to restrain ourselves in using the exclamation point. (It's the strongest emphasis we can give! We can't use it for everything we say! It will lose its effect! So watch it!) Even the example in frame 6 would probably be better punctuated by holding back the exclamation point in some cases: "My God! An avalanche—look out—stand back!" or "My God, an avalanche! Look out, stand back!" or in other ways, depending on what the writer wants to stress most.

8.   Who stuffed that white owl

What punctuation should follow this sentence?

_ _ _ _ _ _ _ _ _ _ _ _ _ _

question mark (It's a direct question.)

9.   What punctuation should follow each sentence in the following exercise? Write E for exclamation point, Q for question mark, or P for period.

_2_ (a)   Where is my box of soap flakes

_1_ (b)   She asked whether anyone had seen the soap flakes

_1_ (c)   We were using them for a snow scene

_1_ (d)   Please give the box to her

_1_ (e)   John, give it to her right now

_1_ (f)   If only Bill hadn't turned on the blower, we might be able to gather them up

_?_ (g)   Whose fault is that

_1_ (h)   Not mine

_ _ _ _ _ _ _ _ _ _ _ _ _ _

(a) Q; (b) P; (c) P; (d) P; (e) E; (f) P; (g) Q; (h) E

10. Besides marking the completion of sentences, the end punctuation in written English often shows the tone or stress. For instance, the questions mark shows the rising voice pitch of a spoken question. There's a great difference between the sound of "John, please give her the box." and "John, please give her the box, won't you?" When we make a question of it, our voice rises in pitch at the end of the sentence. It's certainly a different sound from "John, give her the box!" Isn't it?

    "John, you'll give her the box, won't you?" needs a question mark to show the rising pitch of the *won't you* at the sentence's end. In general, statements or polite commands that end in a brief question (*shouldn't I, didn't he, haven't they,* and the like) are followed by a

    _____ .

- - - - - - - - - - - - - - - - -

    question mark

11. Punctuate each of these sentences:

    (a) Whatever are we going to tell her

    (b) We could say "Would you like us to buy you another box of soap flakes"

    (c) John used the last of the soap flakes, didn't he

- - - - - - - - - - - - - - - - -

    A question mark is used in (a), (b), and (c)

12. What punctuation should follow each sentence in the following exercise? Write E for exclamation point, Q for question mark, or P for period.

    _P_ (a) I have seven cents

    _Q_ (b) Would three pennies and a soda bottle to turn in for deposit help

    _Q_ (c) She wants to know if you could sell any more soda bottles
    _P_

    _P_ (d) Perhaps if John and Bill were to search their pockets, they might have enough money

    _P_ (e) I have some twine and a cork and a test tube of homemade gunpowder—oh, yes, and some fishworms

    _E_ (f) Fishworms In your pocket Ugh

(g)   Diane is coming with us to the store, isn't she

(h)   John asked if you're coming with us

— — — — — — — — — — — — — — — —

(a) P; (b) Q; (c) P; (d) P; (e) P, possibly E; (f) Q, Q, E; (g) Q;
(h) P

13.   Besides its use as an end mark, the question mark has one other minor
function. It can be used to show doubtful accuracy:

Geoffrey Chaucer (1340?–1400) was the son of John Chaucer, a
vintner.

or

Chaucer, born in 1340(?), is the writer whose name comes first to
mind when we think of Middle English.

Notice that in both these examples, the question mark appears within
parentheses. In the first example, additional parentheses aren't necessary, since the information affected by the question mark is itself
within the parentheses.

14.   In other cases, however, the question mark should be enclosed by
parentheses in order to show that it's not an ordinary question mark,
ending a sentence. Rewrite the following uncertain information by
using the parenthetical question mark.

Shakespeare was born on either April 22, or April 23, 1564. The date
most frequently given is April 23.

— — — — — — — — — — — — — — — —

You might have written: Shakespeare was born April 23(?), 1564. (or
something similar)

What is important here is that you indicated doubt about the birthdate
of Shakespeare by (?) following the date.

15.   When no approximate date has been clearly established and the best
guesses show wide variations, it's better to use "about."

Jesus was born about 4 B.C.

rather than:

Jesus was born 4 (?) B.C.

Don't use (?) as a way of avoiding your homework. Use it only when the most authoritative sources are uncertain about the date in question. It's a mark to show that nobody's sure, not that you haven't checked! Except for very personal writing, like your diary or a letter to a close friend, don't use (?) for sarcasm or humor, such as:

I had a lovely (?) time.

Only a friend (?) will find it funny (?).

SELF-TEST

This Self-Test will help you determine how well you have met the objectives for this chapter and whether you are ready to go on to the next chapter. The answers to this Self-Test follow.

Supply the necessary punctuation for the following. Write E for exclamation point, Q for question mark, (Q) for a parenthetical question mark, and P for period.

1. John, why do you always steal Alice's soap flakes when we have a snowstorm to stage

2. Well, I can't use popcorn, can I

3. It's not John's fault   Who else uses soap flakes

4. What a lousy excuse

5. Have you got a better one

6. All right, quiet everybody   Let's calm down a little and try to solve the problem

7. He asked me if I had a better one

8. We don't need a better excuse   We need a better way to make a snow effect   Isn't that the point

9. Here's a scene technician's handbook   I wonder if it has snow-storms

10. What does it say

11. It says here that the father of Greek tragedy was born B.C. 525   They don't seem too sure

12. Ye Gods   Snow effects in Greek tragedy

13. Here it is   Here it is   All we need is to find some confetti, John

14. Does anybody know if Alice has some confetti

Answers to Self-Test

Compare your answers to the Self-Test with those given below. If you answered all questions correctly, go on to the next chapter. If you missed any, review the frames indicated in parentheses following the answers. If you missed several questions, you should probably look back over the whole chapter before going on.

1. Q (frames 8, 10, 11)
2. Q (frames 8, 10, 11)
3. P (frames 2, 3, 4, 5); Q (frames 8, 10, 11)
4. E (frames 6, 7, 10)
5. Q (frames 8, 10, 11)
6. E (frames 6, 7, 10); P (frames 2, 3, 4, 5)
7. P (frames 2, 3, 4, 5)
8. P; P (frames 2, 3, 4, 5); Q (frames 8, 10, 11)
9. P; P (frames 2, 3, 4, 5)
10. Q (frames 8, 10, 11)
11. (Q) (frames 13, 14); P; P (frames 2, 3, 4, 5)
12. E (frames 6, 7, 10); E or Q (frames 8, 10, 11)
13. E; E (frames 6, 7, 10); P (frames 2, 3, 4, 5)
14. Q (frames 8, 10, 11)

CHAPTER THREE

The Comma

The comma is the most versatile and widely used of all punctuation marks. It has so many different uses that all its functions cannot be summed up in a few simple rules. Moreover, it can be used with a greater degree of flexibility than the other punctuation marks, so it offers you more options in your writing. It can help a skillful writer either to speed up or slow down the reader, or to make his or her writing seem either light or heavy in tone.

Because of this variety and flexibility, the comma is not only our most useful punctuation mark but also is the most difficult to master. More so than with any other mark of punctuation, the comma has many optional uses, which depend on the writer's intentions. However, there are a few basic guidelines to follow, and this section will point them out and illustrate them. You will discover that they are far simpler and less confusing than you expected.

Most important, however, is that, instead of trying to memorize a series of comma usage "rules," you should try to discover the underlying principles of punctuation usage, and to see what variations these principles make possible. As a whole, then, this section on comma usage will illustrate the basic premise we started from. Remember? *Punctuation is not something imposed arbitrarily on our writing—it is closely and inherently related to the meaning of what we write.*

More than any other mark, the comma directs the reader, organizes groups of words into meaningful units, and in general makes it easier for a writer to transmit the intended meaning accurately.

Because of the very many different functions the comma has, a unit explaining them all would be very long. Not everyone needs to review all of them. This section will go into detail on the various uses. You may want to hurry over those that are familiar to you, but linger longer on those that seem more troublesome.

OBJECTIVES

When you have completed this chapter, you should be able to:

- use commas in separating independent clauses;
- use commas to separate introductory clauses and phrases from the main clause;
- use commas in separating parts of a series;
- use commas to insure clarity;
- use commas to indicate parenthetical elements in your sentences;
- use commas to show contrasts within your sentences;
- use commas to identify appositives;
- punctuate with commas to stress meaning.

Now we'll go into the various comma uses in detail, illustrate some variations on them, and try to show the reasons for these uses in more technical terms.

1.   One major comma use is to separate independent clauses when those clauses are joined by a conjunction. Technical enough? In plain English, an "independent" clause is a group of words that, by itself, might be a sentence. It can "stand alone," be "independent" of other words. And a "conjunction" is a word used to "conjoin" or connect words, or phrases, or clauses.

So here's our first rule of thumb:

Use a comma to separate long main (independent) clauses when joined by (conjunctions) "and," "but," "or," "nor," and "for."

Clear: Tom came for the book, but I did not let him have it.

Clear: He left the heavy load behind him, for the road ahead was very steep.

Clear: This area has many good roads, and a farmer can easily haul his produce to market.

Exception: The comma is sometimes omitted if the clauses are very short. For example: The women rode and the men walked. They came but they did not stay.

2.   Introductory portions of a sentence that come before the first main clause are usually followed by a comma. The comma becomes a signal to your reader that "Here comes the main message." There are a number of introductory elements that can come before your independent clause.

(a)   Adverb clauses (*not* independent) tell the *how, when, why, where,* or *how much* of what happens in the main clause that follows. For example: <u>After</u> <u>he</u> <u>had</u> <u>finished</u> <u>writing</u>, he turned off the light. <u>Because</u> <u>he</u> <u>hadn't</u> <u>paid</u> <u>his</u> <u>bill</u>, the power company turned off his lights. *Note:* Adverbial clauses have all the necessary parts of a main clause—subject and verb. But adverbial clauses don't make a statement that *means* anything—they cannot "stand alone." For instance, "Before he left" would be a perplexing statement all by itself. "Before he left, he tied his shoes." *does* make sense, as does "He tied his shoes." Adverbial clauses are attached to main clauses.

(b)   Introductory phrases, which may add information, but really don't begin the main statement. For example: <u>After</u> <u>dark</u>, mosquitoes nearly ate us alive. If you leave out the comma here, you confuse the reader; what kind of mosquitoes *are* "dark mosquitoes"? Besides, the main clause becomes meaningless; it no longer could "stand alone." What *does* this mean: "After dark mosquitoes nearly ate us alive"?

(c)   Transitional phrases, which may connect this sentence to the previous one, but aren't part of the main clause. For example: <u>After</u> <u>all</u>, there's no reason to make an issue of it. <u>Clearly</u>, the matter is settled.

So to our next rule of thumb:

Use a comma after introductory clauses and phrases.

> Clear: Because of his effort to escape, his punishment was increased.

> Clear: When the children failed to return from their hike, the frantic parents called the police.

> Clear: Across the lake and on top of a hill, one huge tree stands alone.

> Clear: First of all, we crossed the narrow bridge over the gully.

> Clear: When I was young, I hated school.

> Clear: Say, I wish you could have seen the way the tires spun on the gravel.

> Clear: Throughout the first day and night and well into the night of the second day, the cinders from the forest fire kept raining down.

> Also Clear: Throughout the day the cinders kept falling. (See exception, frame 1)

Now try your hand at it. Write and punctuate an introductory adverb clause that will introduce the main clause provided below. Here are the pieces for your puzzle:

(a) Start each clause with one of these adverbs: *if, when, while, since, although,* or *because.*

(b) Next, add a noun or pronoun: the goat, we, Harry, they, my aunt Emma, etc.

(c) Then add a verb: shouted, whooped, stumbled, smirked, hiccoughed, etc.

(d) And finally, here's the main clause:

the shale slipped, slithered beneath (his, her, our, their, its) feet, and clattered down the mountainside.

Now, on separate paper, put the pieces together to form six sentences that use the six adverbs (a) in introductory adverbial clauses.

— — — — — — — — — — — — — — — —

One result might be: *While the goat smirked and my aunt Emma whooped and hiccoughed,* the shale slipped, slithered beneath their feet and clattered down the mountainside. Or another: *If Harry shouted,* the shale slipped . . . etc. But whatever the combination, the formula should now be apparent—that is, *the adverbial clause is attached to the main clause by a comma. The comma both separates them and signals the beginning of the main clause.*

3. Another important use of the comma is to separate three or more items in a series. When used this way, a comma is always placed before the word "and" in order to keep the meaning clear.

Confusing: The natives ate beans, onions, rice and honey. (Does "rice and honey" mean two separate items, or did they eat the two things mixed together?)

Clear: Men, women, and children crowded into the square.

Clear: The tired, thin, overworked student won a place on the honor roll. (The meaning here would not be made clearer by placing "and" before the third item, "overworked.")

Clear: In the sentimental old ballad, we learn that Frankie caught her lover with another woman, pulled out her pistol, and shot him dead. (introductory adverbial phrase, then a main clause with three parts)

Clear: The city council voted to pave Windberry Street, to in-
stall a swimming pool in the city park, and to lower the
mayor's salary.

Confusing: The airport facilities included numerous hangars, a large
landing strip with taxiways and a restaurant-bar. (That
restaurant-bar could be quite a traffic hazard.)

4.   In its most general function, the comma serves as a signal to provide
clarity and to prevent your reader from misreading your meaning.

Confusing: Inside the room was gaily decorated.
Clear: Inside, the room was gaily decorated.

Confusing: As we ate Grandma told us a story.
Clear: As we ate, Grandma told us a story.

Confusing: Before moving to Portland as a child he lived in California.
Clear: Before moving to Portland, as a child he lived in Califor-
nia. *Or:* Before moving to Portland as a child, he lived in
California. (depends on your meaning)

5.   Commas are used as signals to point out a set of words that are not essential to the meaning of the sentence. The technical term for such elements
is *nonrestrictive;* they do not restrict the sentence's meaning. The rule is:

**Use commas in pairs for setting off nonrestrictive or parenthetical
elements (whether phrases, clauses, or single words).**

Clear: The states which are on the coast have heavy rainfall.
(*No* commas. The full subject is not just "states," but a
particular, restricted group of states: "the states which
are on the coast.")

Clear: Oregon, which is on the coast, has heavy rainfall.

Clear: Trees which are on the coast get plenty of rain.

Clear: His work, on the whole, is satisfactory.

Clear: Our chairman is not here yet; I believe, however, that we
should go ahead with our meeting.

Clear: Our chairman is not here yet; however, I believe that we
should go ahead with our meeting.

Clear: All writers, as a matter of fact, are not crazy. Some of them, on the other hand, are not responsible for their actions.

Clear: Diane Smith, the author of *Brain Surgery Self-Taught*, will speak.

Confusing: Diane Smith, the author of *Brain Surgery Self-Taught* will speak. (Who's speaking? Who's the author?)

Clear: The curtains, stained and tattered, greasily filtered the afternoon sunlight.

Confusing: The curtains, stained and tattered greasily filtered the afternoon sunlight. ("tattered greasily"?)

Clear: Stained and tattered, the curtains greasily filtered the afternoon sunlight.

Clear: The stage, pulled by six sweating horses, drew up at the depot.

Clear: The stage pulled by six sweating horses drew up at the depot.

Note: In these last two sentences, the *meaning makes all the difference.* In the first case, the point is that the stage has arrived; it just happened to have six sweating horses pulling it. In the second, the writer is making a point of those sweating nags; he or she means just that particular stagecoach: the one with six sweating horses, not the other one he just mentioned as having passed by, pulled by six mice with a rat driving. The meaning, again, is signalled by the punctuation.

Try punctuating the following sentences. If a choice of punctuation is possible, notice the difference in meaning.

(a)   Thomas Edison the father of the electric light had little formal education.

(b)   The temples which were built in the reign of Cheops have withstood the weather of centuries.

(c)   Some scientists believe it or not expected the invention of the atomic bomb to make war impossible.

(d)   They were going to try snow or not to reach the peak.

(a)   Thomas Edison, the father of the electric light, had little formal education.

(b) *Either:* The temples, which were built in the reign of Cheops, have withstood the weather of centuries. *Or:* The temples which were built in the reign of Cheops have withstood the weather of centuries. (The second case used "which were built in the reign of Cheops" *restrictively;* the writer means to restrict the subject to those particular temples, not some built in another time. Notice that the *meaning* makes the difference in *your* punctuation.)

(c) Some scientists, believe it or not, expected the invention of the atomic bomb to make war impossible. (Here "believe it or not" is simply inserted into the main statement. It's an interruption, which is signalled by commas at each end. They could be replaced by parentheses.)

(d) They were going to try, snow or not, to reach the peak.

6. Back in frame 2 we dealt with the adverbial clause. A reminder: the adverbial clause is like any other clause in that it consists of at least a subject and a verb. It also includes information that tells the *how, when, why, where,* or *how much* of what happens in the main clause. Examples: *When she got there,* the cupboard was bare. *When the pie was opened,* the birds began to sing.

But introductory adverbial material isn't always an adverbial clause. It may be merely an adverbial *phrase.* These, too, are generally followed by a comma before the main clause. They are formed by a *preposition* followed by a *noun* or *pronoun.* Here are the most common prepositions:

about	beyond	since
above	but	through
across	by	till
after	down	to
against	during	toward
along	ere	under
amid	for	underneath
among	from	until
around	in	unto
at	into	up
before	of	upon
behind	off	with
below	on	within
beneath	over	without
beside	past	like
between	round	except

To form an adverbial phrase, take one of the above prepositions, then add a noun or pronoun. For more phrases, repeat the process:

preposition + object (noun or pronoun). For example: <u>During the time before the eruptions</u>, we could hear the earth rumbling. <u>Beneath the trees beside the brook</u>, the shrubs flowered in profusion. <u>After the war and before the beginnings of mistrust</u>, the nations wanted to disarm.

Now try your hand at it. Remember the formula:

preposition + object + comma + main clause.

_ _ _ _ _ _ _ _ _ _ _ _ _ _ _ _

You might have written any number of introductory adverb phrases. But you should have (a) started with a preposition, then (b) added a noun or pronoun: John, he, old paint, the dog. (This can be repeated and repeated, but too many phrases in a row tend to get confusing.) Your next step is (c) comma, followed by (d) the main clause. Example:

(a) During
(b) the years
(a) after
(b) the fall
(a) of
(b) Rome
(c) , (comma)
(d) there was decreasing regard for the law and increasing reliance on force.

During the years after the fall of Rome, there was decreasing regard for the law and increasing reliance on force.

7. The distinction between phrase and clause lies in the presence of a word that functions as a verb in that particular word group.

(word) + or – (modifiers) + (noun or pronoun) = **phrase**

(word) + or – (modifiers) + (noun or pronoun) + (verb) = **clause**

8. What is the major difference between introductory phrases and the adverb clause?

_ _ _ _ _ _ _ _ _ _ _ _ _ _

The adverb *clause* contains a *verb*.

9.   One of the things that makes the English language fun to use but agony to study is the ease with which words shift in function. Verbs become nouns; nouns become verbs or adjectives; conjunctions become prepositions; prepositions become adverbs; and so on. *Hit,* we say, is a verb. But in *The record will become a hit* it is a noun. *Egg,* we say, is a noun. But when we *egg* on our favorite, or we see an *egg*-shaped object in the sky, it shifts to function as a verb and as an adjective. *But,* of course, is a coordinating conjunction, yet in the sentence *Everyone but the dog went to the cocktail party,* it serves happily as a preposition. *Since* is a preposition in *Since her death, he had worked savagely;* it's an adverb in *Since you went away, nothing seems the same. Until* is a preposition in *Until morning, they watched for Indians;* it's an adverb in *Until morning came, they watched for Indians.*

These shifts in word uses—preposition to conjunction, verb to noun, noun to adjective—emphasize the importance of using punctuation to keep meaning clear in our written English. Other languages have special signals we lack, such as: adding letters to a word that show whether it's the subject or object of a verb, capitalizing a word to show it's a noun, and using words in a certain order that never changes without drastically changing meaning. Our language is more flexible without these rigid rules, but it often demands more care from us in keeping our meaning from being misunderstood.

Writers occasionally use a comma after even a short introductory phrase when it will aid the reader by keeping the meaning clear. Consider:

In the evening twilight shadowed the land.

A comma after the introductory phrase might make the sentence clearer. Write the sentence, including a comma.

In the evening, twilight shadowed the land.

This, of course, is the whole purpose of punctuation: to transmit your thought, whole and clear, to your reader.

10.   Write and punctuate a transitional word or phrase to go with the following main clause. Use one of the following, or think up one of your own: however, moreover, in the first place, in fact, for instance, etc.

_____ he was as stupid a beast as I have ever encountered.

You might have written something like this: In fact, he was as stupid (etc.)

_ _ _ _ _ _ _ _ _ _ _ _ _ _ _

11. Write and punctuate an interjection—a mild exclamation such as: Aha, oh, alas, well, say, ugh, ouch, good grief, look, listen, yes, no—to go with the following sentence:

_____ I have a clue.

_ _ _ _ _ _ _ _ _ _ _ _ _ _ _

Some possible sentences are: Aha, I have a clue. Listen, I have a clue. Yes, I have a clue.

12. Let's summarize the material you have studied so far. Before each of the following sentences, write O if the sentence needs no comma, A if the sentence begins with an adverb clause, B if the sentence begins with one or more long introductory phrases, or with a phrase requiring a comma for the sake of clarity, and C if the sentence begins with either a transitional expression or an interjection. Underline the word in each sentence that should be followed by a comma.

____ (a)   Well I suppose he had it coming to him.

____ (b)   Actually he didn't say why he called.

____ (c)   During the winter we played "Fox and Geese."

____ (d)   During the long and bitterly freezing winter of 1948 we had to have hay for the cattle dropped in by helicopter.

____ (e)   When at last summer came even the grass was ecstatic.

____ (f)   All morning long shadows and sunshine chased one another over the garden.

____ (g)   Unlike caribou cattle must be fed during snowy weather.

_ _ _ _ _ _ _ _ _ _ _ _ _ _ _

_C_ (a)   Well I suppose he had it coming to him.

_C_ (b)   Actually he didn't say why he called.

_O_ (c)   During the winter we played "Fox and Geese." ("During the winter" contains information that restricts the verb "played," and it is really too brief to demand separating it from the main clause.)

_B_ (d)   During the long and bitterly freezing winter of <u>1948</u> we had to have hay for the cattle dropped in by helicopter.

_A_ (e)   When at last summer <u>came</u> even the grass was ecstatic.

_B_ (f)   All morning <u>long</u> shadows and sunshine chased one another over the garden.

_B_ (g)   Unlike <u>caribou</u> cattle must be fed during snowy weather.

13.   The comma, of course, is not the only means of punctuating independent clauses. A series of two or more independent clauses may be punctuated in at least three different ways, depending upon the degree of separation you want to give them. They may be held together fairly tightly by a combination of a conjunction (and, but, or, for, nor) plus a comma, as in

Willy saw the bear,<u> and</u> the bear saw Willy.

They may be held lightly together by using a semicolon:

Willy saw the bear<u>;</u> the bear saw Willy.

Or they may be separated altogether by using a period and capitalizing the next word:

Willy saw the bear.<u> The</u> bear saw Willy.

These three patterns are shown below. Provide the three possible punctuation marks:

(a)   Independent clause __ Independent clause.

(b)   Independent clause __ Independent clause.

(c)   Independent clause __
    and
    but
    or   Independent clause.
    for
    nor

- - - - - - - - - - - - - - - -

(a) period (or semicolon);   (b) semicolon (or period);   (c) comma *plus* conjunction.

14. Remember, the comma is also used to set off _____ elements that begin a sentence.

_ _ _ _ _ _ _ _ _ _ _ _ _ _ _

introductory

15. Show a pattern that will show the placement of punctuation for introductory elements requiring a comma:

_____   _____

_ _ _ _ _ _ _ _ _ _ _ _ _ _ _

Introductory element, Independent clause

16. You have already learned that four kinds of introductory elements coming at the beginning of a sentence require a comma after them. They are

_ _ _ _ _ _ _ _ _ _ _ _ _ _ _ _

Adverb clauses, long phrases, transitional expressions, and interjections.

17. Two commas are also used to set off parenthetical items within a sentence that slightly disturb the flow of meaning. For example:

    (a)   John, you will notice, is embarrassed at being singled out.
    (b)   The butterfly, a Monarch, dived at his head.
    (c)   "Do you suppose," he asked, "there is such a thing as madness among butterflies?"
    (d)   Manuel, however, did not answer at once.
    (e)   John knew, nonetheless, that Manuel's answer would make him feel childish.

All of these sentences contain parenthetical phrases. That is, if the phrases were taken out, the sentence would be essentially the same.
    The parenthetical element (or item) in sentences (a), (b), (c), (d), and (e) is

(a) _____

(b) _____

(c) _____

(d) _____

(e) _____

— — — — — — — — — — — — —

(a) you will notice; (b) a Monarch; (c) he asked; (d) however;
(e) nonetheless

18. Parenthetical expressions in the middle of a sentence are set off by *two*
     commas. In the sentence "No tool that is broken will serve our purposes,"
     the subject of the main clause is

— — — — — — — — — — — — —

No tool

19. The complete predicate of the main clause is

— — — — — — — — — — — — —

will serve our purposes.

20. What group of words is left?

— — — — — — — — — — — — —

that is broken

21. Is *that is broken* parenthetical? (yes/no)

— — — — — — — — — — — — —

no

     To test whether or not an expression is parenthetical, take it out of
the sentence and see whether the sentence is still essentially the same.
No tool will serve our purposes does not at all mean the same thing as
No tool that is broken will serve our purposes. In contrast, *The butterfly
dived at his head* means essentially the same thing as *The butterfly, a
Monarch, dived at his head.*

22. How should you set off an expression that is *not* essential to the meaning of the sentence?

— — — — — — — — — — — — —

with two commas

23. There are many kinds of parenthetical elements. Consider these:
    (a) John, while he had travelled extensively in the Midwest, had never seen the ocean.
    (b) Your mystery book, not your history book, was what I wanted.
    (c) Her version, really, is impossible.
    (d) In Kansas City, Kansas, we watched the sky-diving grandmother's performance.
    (e) On December 7, 1941, they were casually eating breakfast when the announcement came.

    Each parenthetical element is enclosed by ——————————— .

— — — — — — — — — — — — —

two commas

24. Read the following sentences. If the sentence contains *no* parenthetical element, write *X* beside the sentence number. Otherwise, write the words that should be set off by commas on the line that follows the sentence.

    Example: (a) _X_ The boy on the diving board is my favorite.

    —————————

    (b) ___ "Alice" he said "is the prettiest." __he said__

    ___ (a) Dr. Livingstone I presume is your friend. ———————

    ___ (b) August 23 1930 was his favorite day in all history.

    —————————

    ___ (c) A seared and bloody steak not jello was what I ordered.

    —————————

    ___ (d) Mr. Pollux-Castor an old piano-tuner gave me a lithographed card. ———————

_____ (e)   Now the sword that was broken shall be forged anew.

_____

(a) I presume;   (b) 1930;   (c) not jello;   (d) an old piano-tuner;
(e) *X*

25. Notice from the examples you have just seen in the sentences above that dates, addresses, and geographical names are set off, when they occur in mid-sentence, by _____ .

----

commas

26. Parenthetical elements used for contrast are set off by commas. Putting them within commas helps to draw more attention to them, to make them more contrastive, to heighten their meaning. For example:

> My father, *not my mother,* came with me.
> The crowd was booing their coach, *not ours,* after the game.

Give an example of a contrasted parenthetical element set off by commas:

Your answer, not mine, is what's important.

27. Commas are used to set off nonrestrictive appositives in a sentence. *An appositive is a noun or group of words used like a noun that gives another name to a noun in the sentence.* Appositives are either restrictive or nonrestrictive. Restrictive appositives are essential to the meaning of the sentence, whereas nonrestrictive appositives, like parenthetical expressions, can be omitted without distorting the sentence's main idea. Here are some examples of nonrestrictive appositives:

> Mr. Burette, *the glassblower,* came to our house.

> Our house, *that gray stone battlemented castle,* is haunted.

28. Write an appositive phrase to go with the following sentence subject, and then finish the sentence:

My aunt Griselda, _____ , _____

_____ .

— — — — — — — — — — — — — — — —

Possibility: My aunt Griselda, a patient woman, took care of my pet bat and even hatched my spider eggs.

Note: Even when a parenthetical element occurs at the end or beginning of a sentence, it is still set off:

My pet bat was kept by my aunt Griselda, a patient woman.

Remember:

Do set off: *items that can be lifted out of the sentence without destroying it.*

Do **not** set off: *material essential to the sense of the sentence.*

29. Now let's review the rules of comma usage we have applied so far. The comma punctuates (a) independent clauses, (b) introductory elements, (c) parenthetical elements, and (d) items in a series. Show a pattern or patterns to indicate each of these functions of the comma.

(a)

(b)

(c)

(d)

— — — — — — — — — — — — — — —

(a)   <u>(independent clause)</u> , and
but
or   <u>(independent clause)</u>
for
nor

(b)   <u>(introductory element)</u> , <u>(main clause)</u>

(c) <u>(part of main clause)</u> , <u>(parenthetical element)</u> , <u>(rest of main clause)</u> .

(d) <u>(item)</u> , <u>(item)</u> , <u>(item)</u> , and <u>(item)</u> <u>(verb)</u> <u>(rest of sentence)</u> .

So much for abstract patterns. How do they transform into reality? Examples:

        and
        but
(a) (independent clause), or (independent clause)
        for
        nor

(They cancelled the order), but (later they doubled it).

(We gave up fishing), for (the waves were too high).

Note: Each parenthesis contains a clause that could be a sentence by itself.

(b) (introductory element), (main clause)

(Certainly), (the waves were very high).

(On the other hand), (it was a long trip for nothing).

(c) (part of main clause), (parenthetical element), (rest of main clause).

(Fishing for some people), (no doubt), (is more important than staying alive).

("Why you'd want to fish in this weather,") (he grumbled), ("I just plain don't understand.")

(George), (their long-suffering guide), (took no part in the quarrel).

(d) (item), (item), (item), and (item) (verb) (rest of sentence).

(The fire), (the extra firewood), (the axe), and (everything on the beach but their canoe) (had vanished) (by the time they crawled out of the soggy tent next morning).

Reversed:

(That day they) (tried) (to find a higher campsite), (to dry out their clothes), and, (hardest of all), (to keep their tempers). Note the parenthetical insertion "hardest of all."

30. With these patterns and examples to guide you, try your hand at constructing some similar sentences.

31. We should consider a couple of uses of the comma to punctuate items in a series. For some time there was a tendency to omit the comma before the *and* before the last item in a series. But that creates problems in meaning. You need the comma to make a useful distinction between items to be regarded singly and items to be regarded as a group. What is the difference, for example, between these two sentences?

We had coffee, ham and eggs and grapefruit.

We had coffee, ham and eggs, and grapefruit.

_ _ _ _ _ _ _ _ _ _ _ _ _ _ _

In the first sentence each item is regarded as a separate item. In the second sentence the comma makes it clear that *ham and eggs* is a unit. The comma is needed to make a distinction between items regarded singly and items regarded as a group.

32. Normally, what precedes the last item in a series?

_ _ _ _ _ _ _ _ _ _ _ _ _ _ _

a comma followed by *and*

33. What if ham and eggs were the last item in the above sentence? How should the sentence be written then?

_ _ _ _ _ _ _ _ _ _ _ _ _ _ _

We had coffee, grapefruit, and ham and eggs.

34. Nouns aren't the only parts of speech that occur in series. Verbs and phrases can also occur in series, as for example:

> In the park along Riverside Street, and on Bailey Street, children were playing ball, swinging on the swing sets, jumping rope, and chasing squirrels.

Write a sentence in which nouns, verbs, and phrases are used in a series.

_ _ _ _ _ _ _ _ _ _ _ _ _ _ _

Suggestion: Tristan, Anna, and Gretel went hopping, skipping, jumping, and running over the hill, down the lane, and through the woods to a strange little house built entirely of driftwood.

Note: there is no comma *before* the first item in a series, nor *after* the last item.

35. The pattern is

> (piece of sentence) (item), (item), and (item) (rest of sentence).

Write a sentence in which there is no comma before the first item in a series.

_ _ _ _ _ _ _ _ _ _ _ _ _ _ _

Suggestions: He would rather hike, fish, or hunt than eat.

"You are thoughtful, kind, reverent, obedient, and honest," said the scoutmaster.

Try some more sentences of your own built on this pattern.

36. To review comma usage further, punctuate the following passage:

> This is about Mr. Fitch's barn and tells who set it afire setting things afire is arson they say I did it this is the true story I just want to help the police

My cousin Jim asked me to set Mr. Fitch's barn afire and I said
I would not understanding that it might get me into trouble the night
of the fire I went home and talked about Mr. Fitch to my brother
and my cousin Jim had a drink and went out and set fire to the barn
Mr. Nelson said he saw the person setting fire to the barn and knows
it was me or Jim or Mr. Grady said so whoever said it called the police
station across from my house and I was sitting in the front room
when the police came over sixteen was my age at the time of the fire

— — — — — — — — — — — — — — — — —

This is about Mr. Fitch's barn and tells who set it afire. Setting things
afire is arson, they say. I did it. This is the true story. I just want to help
the police.

My cousin Jim asked me to set Mr. Fitch's barn afire, and I said
I would, not understanding that it might get me into trouble. The night
of the fire I went home and talked about Mr. Fitch to my brother
and my cousin Jim, had a drink, and went out and set fire to the barn.
Mr. Nelson said he saw the person setting fire to the barn and knows
it was me. Or Jim or Mr. Grady said so. Whoever said it called the police
station across from my house, and I was sitting in the front room
when the police came. Over sixteen was my age at the time of the fire.

In the sixth line of the above answer, you may have placed a comma
after the word *fire.* A comma there is optional; the phrase is fairly long,
but the passage seems clear enough without the comma.

37. Now, read this version.

This is about Mr. Fitch's barn and tells who set it afire. Setting things
afire is arson. They say I did it. This is the true story. I just want to
help the police.

My cousin Jim asked me to set Mr. Fitch's barn afire, and I said
I would not, understanding that it might get me into trouble. The
night of the fire I went home and talked about Mr. Fitch to my
brother, and my cousin Jim had a drink and went out and set fire to
the barn. Mr. Nelson said he saw the person setting fire to the barn
and knows it was me or Jim. Or Mr. Grady said so. Whoever said it
called the police station across from my house, and I was sitting in
the front room when the police came over. Sixteen was my age at
the time of the fire.

(a)   According to the narrator, who is guilty in the first version?

_____

(b)   Who is guilty in the second version? _____

——————————————————

(a) the narrator;   (b) his cousin, Jim

38. Let's do some more review. The comma is used as punctuation for independent clauses, but such clauses must be joined by *and, but, or, for,* or
nor. That list of the coordinating conjunctions—and, but, or, for, and
nor—illustrates another comma use: it separates items in a series.
Besides separating items in a series and separating independent clauses
joined by a coordinating conjunction, the comma also sets off certain
introductory elements: adverb clauses, long phrases, transitional words,
and interjections. The comma sets off, in addition to these introductory
elements, items known as parenthetical elements. What is the parenthetical element in the last sentence?

——————————————————

in addition to these introductory elements

     If you look back at the sentences in this frame, you'll find that
each one is itself an example of the comma use it describes.

SELF-TEST

This Self-Test will help you determine how well you have met the objectives for this chapter and whether you are ready to go on to the next chapter. The answers to this Self-Test follow.

Punctuate the following sentences.

1. The last time I saw Professor Weatherby he was dancing on the edge of a cliff laughing to himself mumbling something about comma splices and making paper airplanes out of the students' themes.

2. I looked at my watch since it was not yet midnight I could I thought make a phone call without waking anyone

3. No we don't have any Volkswagens but we do have a used Rolls Royce

4. Once a long time ago while I was still a child we lived for a year on the island of Skye

5. The film for more than half the class was a waste of time but the others needed the elementary review

6. Rats should live in a laboratory cage not in the city's sewer systems

7. Anyone going to school full time taking care of a house bringing up four children and tutoring on the side has little time for either crewel embroidery or television

8. Three cases of almond paste five gross of birthday candles five hundred pounds of pastry flour a gross of large cake-boxes and two gross of assorted candy animals made up the baker's order this week.

9. On December 7 1941 hours before the Japanese ambassador delivered the declaration of war the American fleet was sunk at its moorings.

10. Hardly any of the items in that shipment except a few glasses were damaged in the accident.

11. However we count the loss well worth the cost was the victory

12. Oh what a shout arose at this wonderful piece of news unbelievably we were going home at last

13. Doubting while we hoped we asked ourselves if it could be true

14. "How many tons of net weight" he asked "can this new truck carry?"

15. The car an old Chevrolet stalled on the hill

16. It was Harry not Jim who started the fire

Answers to Self-Test

Compare your answers to the Self-Test with those given below. If you answered all questions correctly, go on to the next chapter. If you missed any, review the frames indicated in parentheses following the answers. If you missed several questions, you should probably look over the whole chapter before going on.

1. The last time I saw Professor Weatherby, he was dancing on the edge of a cliff, laughing to himself, mumbling something about comma splices, and making paper airplanes out of the students' themes. (frames 2, 3, 30)

2. I looked at my watch. Since it was not yet midnight, I could, I thought, make a phone call without waking anyone. (frames 2, 5)

3. No, we don't have any Volkswagens, but we do have a used Rolls Royce. (frames 11, 1)

4. Once, a long time ago while I was still a child, we lived for a year on the island of Skye. (frames 2, 5)

5. The film, for more than half the class, was a waste of time, but the others needed the elementary review. (frames 5, 1)

6. Rats should live in a laboratory cage, not in the city's sewer systems. (frames 5, 28)

7. Anyone going to school full time, taking care of a house, bringing up four children, and tutoring on the side has little time for either crewel embroidery or television. (frames 3, 30)

8. Three cases of almond paste, five gross of birthday candles, five hundred pounds of pastry flour, a gross of large cake-boxes, and two gross of assorted candy animals made up the baker's order this week. (frames 3, 30)

9. On December 7, 1941, hours before the Japanese ambassador delivered the declaration of war, the American fleet was sunk at its moorings. (frames 23, 25, 5)

10. Hardly any of the items in that shipment, except a few glasses, were damaged in the accident. (frame 5)

11. However we count the loss, well worth the cost was the victory.
     (frames 1, 4)

12. Oh, what a shout arose at this wonderful piece of news! Unbelievably,
     we were going home at last.   (frames 11, 12)

13. Doubting while we hoped, we asked ourselves if it could be true.
     (frame 2)

14. "How many tons of net weight," he asked, "can this new truck carry?"
     (frames 5, 17)

15. The car, an old Chevrolet, stalled on the hill.   (frame 26)

16. It was Harry, not Jim, who started the fire.   (frame 25)

CHAPTER FOUR

The Semicolon

We have covered, so far, the most commonly used punctuation marks. And in studying them we noted again and again that their function is to make meaning clear for the reader. Periods, question marks, exclamation points, and commas can take care of most of your punctuation needs, but there are other marks that can be used to show even finer shades of meaning. These, too, are closely tied to sentence structure. One of them, the semicolon, is like the comma in that it is used *within* the sentence.

OBJECTIVES

When you have completed this chapter, you should be able to:

- use semicolons to show a related but separate statement within a sentence;
- use the comma, the semicolon, and the period to show degrees of separation between ideas;
- use the semicolon to separate items in series with complex punctuation.

1. The semicolon has two uses: (1) it functions like the period in that it marks independent clauses—word groups that could stand alone as sentences, and (2) it functions like the comma in that it may be used to separate parallel items in a series when the items are complicated by unusual length or by internal punctuation such as a number of commas.

    It is not like the period or the comma in any other ways—that is, the semicolon is *not* followed by a capital letter, as the period is; it is *not* used to separate certain dependent clauses or introductory elements from the rest of the sentence, as the comma is.

2.   The semicolon is like the period only in that it separates word groups that could

——————————————

stand alone as sentences.

3.   It is like the comma in that it separates parallel items in a series, and it is used when

——————————————

the items are complicated by unusual length or internal punctuation.

4.   Whether you use a period or a semicolon in a particular place depends on how close a tie you want to make between the two ideas. A period makes the greatest separation; and so, to separate two grammatically complete word groups, you mark the end of each group with a

————————————— .

——————————————

period

5.   A semicolon makes a closer bond than a period. So, to combine two grammatically complete word groups which are related, a writer marks

the end of the first group with a ————————————— .

——————————————

semicolon

6.   Write the sentence that would result if you decided to combine these two closely related ideas.

The moose is very like the deer.

Its horns drop off when spring is near.

——————————————

The moose is very like the deer; its horns drop off when spring is near.

7.   What sentences would result if you decided to separate these two some-
      what divergent ideas by changing the punctuation?

      The hen has no teeth; Rhode Island Reds, as a rule, are easily
      hypnotized.

- - - - - - - - - - - - - - - - - - -

      The hen has no teeth. Rhode Island Reds, as a rule, are easily hypno-
      tized. (Separation, here, certainly improves the meaning.)

8.   Supply punctuation between the independent clauses in the following
      sentences. (*Remember:* an independent clause is a grammatically com-
      plete idea; it can stand alone as a sentence.) Be careful; some of the
      sentences may contain only one grammatically complete idea. In the
      space provided, write the words that appear before and after the punc-
      tuation mark you supply.

      (a)   He used to walk a lot sometimes, walking over the bridges in the
             evenings, he thought of Kathy.

      (b)   We were growing desperately tired toward nightfall we decided we
             had to rest, at least for a little while.

      (c)   If only she had not lost the ring, she would still be able to vanish
             at will.

      (d)   Bill would have been able to finish his amplifier if only he had not
             mislaid a resistor.

      (e)   He was weak his neuromuscular coordination was gone his mental
             activity was confused.

(f)   The winner was dumfounded how could a driver with so grave a
      handicap have stayed in the race to the end?

_ _ _ _ _ _ _ _ _ _ _ _ _ _ _ _

(a)   Possibilities: lot. Sometimes, walking
                       lot; sometimes, walking
                       sometimes. Walking
                       sometimes; walking
(b)   Possibilities: tired. Toward
                       tired; toward
                       nightfall. We
                       nightfall; we
(c)   no punctuation needed
(d)   no punctuation needed
(e)   Possibilities: weak; his . . . gone; his
                       weak. His . . . gone. His
                       weak. His . . . gone; his
                       weak; his . . . gone. His
(f)   dumfounded. How (The semicolon would not be very good in this
      example, since the last clause is phrased as a question and since
      the separation makes both sentences more emphatic.)

Note: in (a), (b), and (c) the punctuation provides many options for
emphasis and, therefore, slight changes in meaning.

9.   Time for a refresher. What is an independent clause the equivalent of?

_ _ _ _ _ _ _ _ _ _ _ _ _ _

      a sentence

10.   Phrased as a statement, how is a sentence marked at its end?

_ _ _ _ _ _ _ _ _ _ _ _ _ _

      with a period

11.   You can test whether a particular group of words should be marked
      with a period by reading it aloud and separating it from the rest of the

material you're writing. Can the group of words following the first period stand alone? (Yes/No) _____

Mumford believes that these buildings should be a play of light and shadows. Formed in such a way that they produce a plastic effect.

_____

no

12. Now consider these expressions. Do they express a complete idea? (Yes/No)

(a)   He used to walk   _____

(b)   A lot sometimes   _____

(c)   Walking over the bridges in the evening   _____

(d)   He thought of Kathy   _____

_____

(a) yes; (b) no; (c) no; (d) yes

13. Select two independent clauses found in this sentence.

We were growing desperately tired toward nightfall we decided to rest, at least for a little while.

(a)   _____

(b)   _____

_____

(a)   We were growing tired.
(b)   We decided to rest.

14. What are the three independent clauses found in these words?

He was weak his neuromuscular coordination was gone his mental activity was confused

(a)   _____

(b)   _____

(c)   _____

_____

(a) He was weak.
(b) His neuromuscular coordination was gone.
(c) His mental activity was confused.

These clauses are stripped to the essentials. Hardly a word can be removed without changing not only the meaning but the grammatical completeness of each clause.

15. When two grammatically complete ideas are closely related, how may they be combined in a single sentence?

— — — — — — — — — — — — — —

by punctuating the end of the first clause with a semicolon instead of a period

16. A semicolon shows a close relationship between what?

— — — — — — — — — — — — — —

the two independent clauses it separates

Remember that the semicolon functions like the period in that it marks independent clauses. It also functions like the comma in that it may be used to separate parallel items in a series when the items are complicated by unusual length or internal punctuation. Ordinarily, the comma is used to separate words or phrases in a series, but sometimes problems arise, as when the independent clauses contain commas.

17. Consider:

Sweetheart, would you kick and scream and yell and throw a fit if you knew that I am planning to take my barbells; the last twelve issues of *Playboy;* your typewriter, complete with a ream of typing paper and some E-Z-Rase; last year's checkstubs, a calculator, and the income tax forms; my briefcase, which won't hold all of this but may help a little; some of that smoked salmon and a pound of smoked cheese, with cutting-board; my accordion, and the tape-recorder to help my practicing; and maybe a couple of novels along on our vacation?

The semicolons in this paragraph separate clearly each group of items in a complex list. Commas separating the groups would be lost among the commas within each group.

18.   Punctuate this sentence:

From the window of his bedroom over the garage Ephraim could see his father's 1952 Plymouth station wagon its right-hand door sagging his brother's small and weedy corn patch his mother's wheelbarrow the hoe and shovel lying across it a locust tree the end of the brick walk that ran between the garage and the house and a blackened scar in the grass left from the Guy Fawkes' Day bonfire when he and his brothers had run like madmen wild with sparklers in the November mist.

_____

From the window of his bedroom over the garage Ephraim could see his father's 1952 Plymouth station wagon, its right-hand door sagging; his brother's small and weedy corn patch; his mother's wheelbarrow, the hoe and shovel lying across it; a locust tree; the end of the brick walk that ran between the garage and the house; and a blackened scar in the grass, left from the Guy Fawkes' Day bonfire, when he and his brothers had run like madmen, wild, with sparklers in the November mist.

19.   Could you omit the comma after bonfire and the comma after wild? (Yes/No) _____

_____

Yes

20.   Let's summarize what we've learned about the semicolon so far. Primarily, the semicolon punctuates closely related independent clauses. It can also be used for complicated lists such as those in frames 17 and 18. This second function of the semicolon is useful to know—sometime you may find yourself floundering in a swamp of items and commas, and *need* some firm, solid semicolons to use as anchors—but it is more important that you understand completely how to punctuate

independent clauses, since every sentence you write must, by definition, contain one or more independent clauses.

21.   Study the familiar patterns below. Thus far we have considered three patterns of punctuation for independent clauses:

(a)   (grammatically complete idea). (grammatically complete idea).

(b)   (grammatically complete idea); (grammatically complete idea).

and
but
(c)   (grammatically complete idea), or (grammatically complete idea).
for
nor

The third pattern creates the closest tie. (See frame 1, Chapter 3 if you need to review.) Here, two grammatically complete ideas are combined with a comma and a word such as nor, or, for, but, and (coordinate conjunctions), to create a compound sentence.

22.   The two sentences below are closely related, and for a good, fluent reading they could be combined. Make a compound sentence out of them, joining them with a comma plus *and.*

Years of political life had given the President a sense of the

something-has-gone-awry. The carefully turned phrases of the

advisers had made that sense jangle like an alarm bell.

— — — — — — — — — — — — — —

Years of political life had given the President a sense of the something-has-gone-awry, and the carefully turned phrases of the advisers had made that sense jangle like an alarm bell.

23.   Another example:

Smokers of one genetic pattern seldom developed lung cancer. Those of another pattern almost invariably did so.

Although these last two sentences are not quite so interdependent as the previous pair, they are related in subject matter and structure, and the comparison they express makes us feel the need for a closer tie between them.

24. How should the sentence in frame 23 be joined? Write out the full sentence:

_____

With a semicolon: Smokers of one genetic pattern seldom developed lung cancer; those of another pattern almost invariably did so.

25. Here are two more sentences to consider:

Some freight-loading equipment has, over long period of use proven to be almost indispensable in time-saving, and thus it has become essential in cost-saving for freight-handling operations. None of this equipment, however, has been able to replace manpower in certain applications, and this is especially true where odd-lot shipments have been combined in one container.

Should the two sentences be combined? (Yes/No) _____ . Give your reasons.

_____

No. The way you may put this may differ, but here are two reasons: (1) the sentences are not closely enough related to warrant such a tie, and (2) both sentences already contain two independent clauses, so that the structure, further compounded by semicolons, would become ponderous and unwieldy. As they are now punctuated, divided by a period and capitalization, they separate into two distinct topics: the first deals with the value of machinery, the second with the necessity for manpower. Again: remember, punctuation should support *meaning!*

26. Fill in the appropriate punctuation (comma, semicolon, etc.) for each of the following pairs of sentences:

(a) By the same token, if a heavy object is set in motion it will be very

hard to stop _ for instance, a worker on the construction of a space station who happened to get in the way of a slowly moving steel beam and was pinned against the structure by it would be crushed to death by its inertial motion, despite its weightlessness.

(b)   The thing was written smoothly enough, it seemed to me when I
reread it in his office— but I went back and checked my next to
last draft.

(c)   Though I had been careful enough in checking the spelling, I had
omitted a line when I retyped one page— and I had to stay past
quitting time to get it into today's mail.

(d)   The experience was— for both of us— annoying in the extreme—
for we both had other plans that were upset by this delay.

— — — — — — — — — — — — — —

(a) semicolon; (b) comma; (c) comma; (d) comma, comma, comma

27.   As you may have noticed in the above examples, *for* and *but* function
as several parts of speech, not just as coordinating conjunctions. Look
at these sentences to see how many different ways *for* and *but* can be
used:

He built the thing himself; he did it *for* money.

But what's it *for?*

For! What do you think it's *for?*

That's not *for* me to say, *for* I don't understand machinery.

Well, *for* example, when you push this button the machine begins
eating dirt and playing *The St. James Infirmary Blues:* it's a quick,
musical way to excavate *for* a basement. Or you could, *for* instance,
throw this switch *for* dimming the lights; that automatically starts
its Martini-mixing circuits, and it mixes seventeen and then asks *for*
more orders, *but* it can be programmed *for* as many as you wish.

(a)   How many times was *for* used in these sentences? _____

(b)   How many times was *for* used as a coordinating conjunction? _____

— — — — — — — — — — — — — —

(a) twelve; (b) one (line 4 ". . . , for I don't understand machinery.")

28.   Remember, when it is functioning as a coordinating conjunction, *for*
joins an independent clause to _____
and is punctuated by a _____ .

— — — — — — — — — — — — — —

an independent clause; comma

29. An independent clause is the equivalent of a _____ in that it can stand alone as a grammatically complete verbal expression of thought.

_____

a sentence

30. A sentence containing two or more independent clauses is called a *compound* sentence. You may form a compound sentence by joining independent clauses with one of the five coordinating conjunctions: _____
_____ .

_____

and, but, or, for, nor

31. Which mark of punctuation precedes the conjunction?

_____

a comma

32. The comma is not the only mark used to show that you've joined two independent clauses; a writer may omit the coordinating conjunction and separate the clauses with what?

_____

a semicolon

33. The semicolon calls for a longer pause, a more emphatic break, than the comma does; what means a still longer stop, a more complete break than either the comma or the semicolon provides?

_____

a period

34. Punctuate the following pairs or groups of clauses in the way that seems most appropriate.

(a) You might become uninterested in the course___ you might feel that you're doing the same thing again and again.

(b) Although he played several different characters in the plays that season___ each one seemed to be an individual___ they were not at all like each other.

(b) A writing course spread out over three years not only helps the student in his other classes___ but it allows him time to develop his writing in ways that would not show up in his first year.

(d) If you take all your writing work as a freshman___ you might feel that you're doing the same thing over and over again___ or in later years you might feel that you somehow have missed something.

(e) England's foremost actor___ Lord Lawrence Olivier___ has shown a mastery in all kinds of dramatic media___ he has won acclaim for his work in film___ in television___ and in stage roles.

(f) The curriculum is designed to spread the work in science electives over two or more years___ it does not have to be taken all at once.

— — — — — — — — — — — — — — — —

(a) A semicolon is probably best, since the clauses are related in content and structure.

(b) A comma after "season" indicates an introductory adverbial clause; a semicolon is appropriate after "individual," since the content of the final independent clause develops ideas in the first one. However, if you want to make it more emphatic, you might separate it from the first by a period.

(c) A comma begins the signal that the coordinating conjunction *but* completes.

(d) A comma after "freshman" again signals an introductory dependent clause; a comma after "again" with *or* joins the independent clauses.

(e) Commas on either side of "Lord Lawrence Olivier" show it is an appositive, meaning the same as the words that come before it; a semicolon after "media" shows that the two independent clauses are similar in content; two more commas are used in the series ending the sentence.

(f) A semicolon here connects (and separates) two independent clauses with similar content.

35. It is perfectly "legal" to use a semicolon or even a period before a co-ordinating conjunction when you want to emphasize a strong contrast or create a certain effect in transition. For example, compare the effect of different punctuation in the following sentence:

> I used every kind of argument I could think of and talked to him hours on end, but he wouldn't pay any attention, and finally he did it his own way.

> I used every kind of argument I could think of and talked to him hours on end; but he wouldn't pay any attention, and finally he did it his own way.

> I used every kind of argument I could think of and talked to him hours on end. But he wouldn't pay any attention; finally he did it his own way.

> I used every kind of argument I could think of and talked to him hours on end, but he wouldn't pay any attention. And finally he did it his own way.

All of these are legitimate uses of punctuation; and each makes what is said slightly different, because the punctuation shifts the *emphasis* of what is said. The words are the same, but by shifting emphasis you can change, sometimes only slightly, the meaning you want the words to carry to your reader.

Look back at the sentences in frame 34. Try using some imaginative punctuation on them to see what different effects you can create by shifting emphasis.

36. It's time to point out a pitfall. So far in working with the semicolon you may have noticed this fact: to join two independent clauses with a coordinating conjunction you must also use a comma. It takes *both* the comma *and* the coordinating conjunction to complete the connection. However, the semicolon is enough by itself. Unlike the semicolon, the comma *cannot* be used *alone* to join two independent clauses. When it is so misused, it is called a *comma splice.* Ordinarily, a comma splice makes a mess of your meaning. How? Generally speaking, it conveys *no* meaning; it does none of the things that a clear signal like a semicolon, a period, or a comma-plus-coordinating-conjunction gives the reader. It is a splice, in that it joins two sets of statements together, but it fails to "splice," (or join) in that it does not show the relationship of those ideas to each other. It is thus a joint with little or no meaning. Look over these examples:

Comma splice:
>These abnormal people in turn would watch us, they would call us abnormal and think of themselves as right.

Revised:
>These abnormal people in turn would watch us; they would call us abnormal and think of themselves as right.

Or:
>These abnormal people in turn would watch us, and they would call us abnormal and think of themselves as right.

Or:
>These abnormal people in turn would watch us. They would call us abnormal and think of themselves as right.

Or:
>Since they think of themselves as right, these abnormal people in turn would watch us, and they would call us abnormal.

Which of the above seems the best revision? As always, it depends on the *meaning* you wish to convey to your reader. But whatever the meaning, the revisions share the virtue of being clearer. The comma splice only confuses, since, *by itself,* the comma is *not* a signal that two independent clauses are joined. The revised sentences use punctuation in ways that keep the signals, and therefore the meaning, clear.

SELF-TEST

This Self-Test will help you determine how well you have met the objectives for this chapter and whether you are ready to go on to the next chapter. The answers to this Self-Test follow.

Punctuate the following sentences:

1. For over a century Colt has produced firearms it helped supply this country's military needs during five wars.

2. It's a yearly pattern each summer the East faces brownouts because of air-conditioning demands and each winter it faces brownouts because of heating demands.

3. The President failed to understand the resistance to his program and so he continued to promote it failing also to notice that his promotion only increased the people's dissatisfaction.

4. Miles away from the downed airmen floating in a current that carried minute traces of blood from their wounds swam a Great White shark.

5. To Prince Valiant the castle looked impregnable moat drawbridge turrets and keep had been laid out and built by a master hand.

6. While it seemed only a slender possibility that the cavalry might survive the attack Custer had no options he could only form a defense and wait for reinforcements that would never arrive in time meanwhile the Sioux were massing for the final charge.

7. The two pilots filed the same flight plan the only difference being their arrival times.

8. "Why is it" he puzzled "that the price of a pound of coffee keeps going down but the price of a cup of coffee keeps going up?"

9. The protesters against nuclear power were gaining public support for an accident at one plant showed the dangers involved.

Answers to Self-Test

Compare your answers to the Self-Test to those given below. If you answered all questions correctly, go on to the next chapter. If you missed any, review the frames indicated in parentheses following the answers. If you missed several questions, you should probably look back over the whole chapter before going on.

1. For over a century Colt has produced firearms; it helped supply this country's military needs during five wars.   (frames 5, 14, 15, 19, 20)

2. It's a yearly pattern; each summer the East faces brownouts because of air-conditioning demands, and each winter it faces brownouts because of heating demands.   (frames 5, 15, 19)

3. The President failed to understand the resistance to his program, (or ;) and so he continued to promote it, failing also to notice that his promotion only increased the people's dissatisfaction.   (frames 20, 21, 34)

4. Miles away from the downed airmen, floating in a current that carried minute traces of blood from their wounds, swam a Great White shark. (frames 1, 8, 11, 12)

5. To Prince Valiant the castle looked impregnable; moat, drawbridge, turrets, and keep had been laid out and built by a master hand. (frames 5, 15, 19)

6. While it seemed only a slender possibility that the cavalry might survive the attack, Custer had no options; he could only form a defense and wait for reinforcements that would never arrive in time. Meanwhile, the Sioux were massing for the final charge.   (frames 19, 20)

7. The two pilots filed the same flight plan, the only difference being their arrival times.   (frames 9, 12)

8. "Why is it," he puzzled, "that the price of a pound of coffee keeps going down, but the price of a cup of coffee keeps going up?" (frames 19, 20)

9. The protesters against nuclear power were gaining public support, for an accident at one plant showed the dangers involved.   (frames 19, 20, 26)

CHAPTER FIVE

The Colon and the Dash

In this chapter we will cover how to use the colon and the dash. A colon places strong emphasis on what is to follow: a formal list, a quotation, or an amplification. Like all punctuation marks, the colon should not be over-used, and it should never be used without a reason. While the colon is a rather formal punctuation mark, the dash is comparatively informal. It is only used in formal writing when (1) it sets off compound appositives in the middle of a sentence, or (2) it emphasizes and sets off other parenthetical material.

OBJECTIVES

When you have completed this chapter, you should be able to:

- use the colon to signal a formal list;
- use the colon to indicate a compound appositive in an informal list;
- use a colon to signal a long quotation;
- use the colon to show emphasis;
- use the colon to introduce a brief quotation;
- use the colon in punctuating times;
- use the colon for business letter salutations;
- use the colon in book titles;
- use the colon in Biblical references;
- use dashes to set off a compound appositive when it occurs in midsentence;
- use dashes to create stronger emphasis for parenthetical material;
- type the dash correctly.

1. A formal list is indicated by phrases such as *the following, as follows, these.* Here's an example of a formal list.

Because of extreme fire danger, the following forest areas have been closed to public entry: the Tillamook burn area, the Yacolt burn, and the St. Helens burn.

2.   Now write a sentence that contains a *formal* list.

_ _ _ _ _ _ _ _ _ _ _ _ _ _ _

Sample answer: When opened to the public, these areas can be used by travellers, but they *must* carry the fire equipment listed as follows: an axe, a long-handled shovel, and a metal bucket.

3.   An informal list occurs without words such as *the following, as follows, these,* and without a colon. An example of an informal list is:

David told his friends to buy American, but he owned a small Toyota truck, a Volkswagen bus, a Triumph sport car, and a Honda motor-cycle.

4.   Write a sentence containing a list that is *not* formal.

_ _ _ _ _ _ _ _ _ _ _ _ _ _ _

Sample answer: In her beachbag she carried an enormous pink towel, a box of chocolates, a bottle of suntan oil, a pair of manicure scissors and a nailfile, a bottle of nail polish in a color called Cellini Bronze, and a volume of plays by Ionesco.

5.   Rewrite the main clause of your sentence with an informal list, first using *the following,* then using *these.*

_ _ _ _ _ _ _ _ _ _ _ _ _ _ _

Sample answers:

In her beachbag she carried *the following:* an enormous pink towel, (etc.).

In her beachbag she carried *these* items: an enormous pink towel, (etc.).

6. From your study of comma uses in Chapter 3, you may remember the term **appositive**. An example used was *The butterfly, a Monarch, dived at my head.* Here *a Monarch* is an appositive for *The butterfly;* they mean the same thing. You may have noticed that using the colon to punctuate a formal list involves a similar situation. The colon acts almost like an equal sign. Look at these, for instance, from previous sentences:

> fire equipment listed as follows: an axe, a long-handled shovel, and a metal bucket

> the following: an enormous pink towel, (etc.)

> these items: an enormous pink towel, (etc.)

When you want to make it clear that you are giving your reader the series of parts that make up a whole, the colon becomes the equal sign in the formula $(x = A + B + C)$.

> I have three shirts: a white one for dress, a knitted one for leisure, and a wreck I wear for painting. (shirts = 1, 2, and 3)

> Three of his faults troubled her most: his untidiness, his sloppy eating habits, and his constantly telling unpleasant truths. (faults = untidiness, sloppy eating habits, telling unpleasant truths)

In these cases the colon signals your reader that you are about to amplify or exemplify what you've just said (as in its most common use in this book); for example:

> He lay as comfortably as he could on the splintery cross-pieces of the hatch-cover, and, though the pitching-motion of the tossing seas made his queasiness return, he still could not stop the parade of food-memories that trooped through his mind: steaks steaming in mushroom sauce, flanked by white mountains of butter-dripping whipped potatoes; gravies of all kinds and colors; lima beans with slivered almonds; tart Chianti, garlic bread, the thyme-oregano smells of richly sauced spaghetti, powdered over with grated parmesan and romano; melons oozing sweetness, drifts of whipped cream over juice-drenched strawberries.

Why is a colon used after the second independent clause (ending with "mind") even though a formal list is not signalled?

_ _ _ _ _ _ _ _ _ _ _ _ _ _ _

After the independent clauses and the colon comes a series of items that *equal* (amplify) "the parade of food-memories that trooped through his mind."

7.   Another use of the colon is to signal the beginning of a long quotation. When a quotation exceeds four lines, it is usually indented both from left and right margins, and quotation marks are omitted, as below:

> Fellow stockholders, it is appropriate at this time to cite the advice given by the company's founder, J. Cash Debenture:
>
> > Buy low and sell high, gentlemen; that is the secret of it all. No matter how many computers you own, how many corporate boards you sit on, how many Swiss bank-accounts you have, how many Senators call you by your first name, the principle remains true. Violate that principle, and you're out of business!
>
> And, gentlemen, those are words to live by!

8.   In the chapter on the semicolon we examined ways that punctuation can add emphasis. You can also make the colon work for you as an emphasis-pointer. Where you might ordinarily use a comma before a brief appositive, a colon will be more striking, will attract more attention, and so will be more emphatic. For instance:

> The reaction of the crowd signified only one thing: apathy.

> This political party has energy, ideas, and experience; it lacks only one thing necessary to win the election: a candidate.

9.   Another specific use of the colon is in introducing a formal quotation. In this situation, the colon is used in place of a comma. For example:

> (a)   Clem Thomas, interviewed separately, said the following: "The people who have come out for Richard Nixon have done so as a matter of principle."

(b)   Speaking on the occasion of the third anniversary of the society's establishment, its founder said this: "We have seen the great promise of our dreams fulfilled. The tree has borne good fruit."

But:

(c)   Clem Thomas, interviewed separately, said "The people who have come out for Richard Nixon have done so as a matter of principle."

(d)   Speaking on the occasion of the third anniversary of the society's establishment, its founder said "We have seen the great promise of our dreams fulfilled. The tree has borne good fruit."

In (a) and (b) the colon serves as you have seen it do before; it separates the thing from the examples of the thing. It acts like an equal sign. In (a), the words "the following" are equal to what comes after them, the quotation itself. The same is true in (b), where "this" equals the quotation. In (c) and (d) the whole quotation becomes part of the independent clause; the quotation is the object of the verb "said," just as in these sentences:

He said his prayers.

George said "Goodbye and good luck."

They said they were sorry.

In a sentence of your own creation, use a colon in formally introducing the following: Mark Antony said "I come to bury Caesar, not to praise him."

———————————————

One possibility: Mark Antony, speaking from the Senate floor, uttered these words: "I come to bury Caesar, not to praise him." (Note that the period goes within the quotation marks. We will look at this more closely in Chapter 8.)

10.   We have seen how the colon signals expansion of an idea, a sort of multiple appositive. It may also separate two main clauses when the second clause expands upon, clarifies, or explains the first, as for example:

(a)   And they learned that the chain of fibroin was fully extended: that is, the atoms were in as nearly a straight line as the angles of the bonds between them would permit.

(b)   His is the familiar attitude which discontented writers assume toward the age they live in: the good old days were better.

To practice this colon use, write a sentence in which you say that *Heinrich Schliemann was at last successful.* Amplify this by explaining what he did—that *he uncovered the ruins of the city of Troy.*

_ _ _ _ _ _ _ _ _ _ _ _ _ _ _ _ _

You might have said something like this: After a long series of disappointments, Schliemann at last succeeded: what he uncovered this time was Troy.

11.   Besides its functions as introducer of lists, quotations, and explanatory clauses, the colon is used in these cases:

(a)   in expressing time when numerals are used:

He caught the 1:40 train.
He caught the train at 1:40 P.M.

(b)   after the salutation in a business letter:

Dear Sir:
Dear Ms. Smith:

(c)   between title and subtitle, even when no colon appears on the title page of the work:

The Dangerous Sex: The Myth of Feminine Evil

(d)   between chapter and verse of a Biblical reference:

in Luke 6:20–27

Punctuate this passage:

I had caught the 10 40 and was happily engrossed in rereading *The Price of the Prairie A Story of Kansas* when the severe-looking lady in the seat across from me admonished me. "Remember Jeremiah 51 63," she said. Startled I got out my *Oxford Annotated Bible* and looked up the verse. It read "When you finish reading this book, bind a stone to it, and cast it into the midst of the Euphrates." By way of thanking her for becoming involved I complimented her for she possessed three things I had always wanted an excellent memory the ability to talk easily to strangers and an antique brooch.

—————————————————

I had caught the 10:40 and was happily engrossed in rereading *The Price of the Prairie: A Story of Kansas* when the severe-looking lady in the seat across from me admonished me. "Remember Jeremiah 51:63," she said. Startled, I got out my *Oxford Annotated Bible* and looked up the verse. It read: "When you finish reading this book, bind a stone to it, and cast it into the midst of the Euphrates." By way of thanking her for becoming involved, I complimented her, for she possessed three things I had always wanted: an excellent memory, the ability to talk easily to strangers, and an antique brooch.

12. From the earlier material on the colon you will remember that a compound appositive is a list of items, all of which are parts of the thing they expand on or amplify, as in this example:

George owned several vehicles: a Ford truck, a snowmobile, a moped, and a Mercedes limousine.

But notice that this group of appositives comes at the end of the sentence. If the colon is used like an equal sign, then what appears before and after the colon must be equal. In the case above, "vehicles" = truck, snowmobile, moped, and limousine. The end of the sentence is the end of the equation.

Dashes put the equation in midsentence; this allows for more material to come after it. For example:

George owned several vehicles—a Ford truck, a snowmobile, a moped, and a Mercedes limousine—which kept him constantly broke.

As you can see, the colon won't work here. The sentence is only *interrupted* by the appositive, not *ended* by it. Commas are also used to set off appositives, but they won't work here; there are already commas, needed to separate the items in the compound appositive. Without confusing the reader you can say "Baby June, his sister, was a sweet child." The single appositive, "his sister," is set off by commas. But if we punctuate our earlier sample sentence with commas alone, we create a different meaning:

George owned several vehicles, a Ford truck, a snowmobile, a moped, a Mercedes limousine, which kept him constantly broke.

Maybe it *was* the Mercedes that kept him broke, but the meaning has certainly shifted from the statement that his whole fleet of vehicles was responsible by creating a rather confusing sentence that blames the Mercedes more than anything else. If you set off the compound appositive with dashes, it's easier for your reader to grasp your meaning.

13. Here's another example:

> Travellers in the fire-danger areas must carry certain equipment—axe, shovel, and metal bucket—at all times.

The group of words set off by the dashes is

____ (a)   an independent clause

____ (b)   a special group that does not fit any rules governing punctuation

____ (c)   a compound appositive

____ (d)   a sudden break in thought

- - - - - - - - - - - - - - - -

(c)   a compound appositive

14. And yet another example. Punctuate the following:

> When he considered all the alternatives common stocks municipal bonds commodity futures tax-free annuities and gold bars that had been explained to him, his mind reeled with facts and figures.

- - - - - - - - - - - - - - - -

When he considered all the alternatives—common stocks, municipal bonds, commodity features, tax-free annuities, and gold bars—that had been explained to him, his mind reeled with facts and figures. (Here the appositive is in the middle of an introductory adverb clause, which is followed by a comma before the main clause.)

15. And one more time!

> The test required that he demonstrate skill in all the strokes Australian crawl elementary back stroke breast stroke and side stroke which the course had covered.

- - - - - - - - - - - - - - - -

The test required that he demonstrate skill in all the strokes—
Australian crawl, elementary back stroke, breast stroke, and side
stroke—which the course had covered.

16. Dashes can also be used to create emphasis. They break the flow of the
sentence and make your reader pause to take notice. Used thus, dashes
work like a parenthesis, only stronger. Consider these two sentences:

The hopes he expressed for the future—and they were never more
than hopes—had been taken to be his promises.

The hopes he expressed for the future (and they were never more
than hopes) had been taken to be his promises.

17. What words should be set off by dashes in the following sentence?

What he failed to realize about the Tonight Show audience millions
of people each night, who tuned into and out of the program as the
guests came and went was that their income-level exceeded the
national average.

————————————————————

millions of people each night, who tuned into and out of the program
as the guests came and went

18. Supply dashes in punctuating the following sentence:

What was important in knowing information about audience income

nobody ought to be more aware than he, it was certain was that the

product being sold had to be pitched at an audience that could

afford it.

————————————————————

What was important in knowing information about audience income—
nobody ought to be more aware than he, it was certain—was that the
product being sold had to be pitched at an audience that could
afford it.

19. One final note: in typing, the dash is formed by two hyphens (--), not
    one (-). There is *no* space either before or after the dash, nor between
    hyphens.

    Correct: blah, blah, blah--more or less--blah, blah

    Incorrect: blah, blah, blah -- more or less -- blah, blah

SELF-TEST

This Self-Test will help you determine how well you have met the objectives for this chapter and whether you are ready to go on to the next chapter. The answers to this Self-Test follow.

Punctuate the following:

1. When leaving the aircraft check that you have the following items ready your passport your health certificate (if travelling from certain areas which the steward will announce) your baggage claim tickets and your boarding pass.

2. Although he might have bought much more duty-free merchandise and still have been within the legal limits Henry made only three purchases a bottle of Scotch for his brother a commemorative china plate for his mother and a hand-knit cashmere tam for his little sister Baby June.

3. As he waited in the terminal for the 12 05 flight to arrive the words of the 23rd Psalm kept going through his mind.

4. Before going on to show how Hamlet's advice to the actors fits in with the rest of the play I'd like to remind you of what he said

    Speak the speech I pray you as I pronounced to you trippingly
    on the tongue. But if you mouth it as many of your players do
    I'd as lief the town crier spoke my lines.

    Obviously maybe too obviously these words are as appropriate today as when Shakespeare who was an experienced actor himself wrote them for his own fellow-actors to hear.

5. Nobody seemed to notice that he'd forgotten his prepared speech or maybe nobody cared. At least it worried one person himself.

6. Alice wondered why her brothers had always made changing a tire such a big deal when it was such a simple process jack up the car take off the flat put on the spare and let the car down again. But then the traffic started getting heavier and coming closer and closer the rain

began freezing as it hit the car and darkness fell faster than she could remember its ever doing before.

7.   When he woke from his daydream Bob Cratchit found he had written the following:

Dear Mr. Scrooge

I used up all the coal in trying to keep warm and then I burned the ledgers. There's only this last scrap of paper left but there are three remaining pieces of furniture my stool this desk and the bookcase. When they're gone I go.

Hoping you have a very Merry Christmas I am

The unfinished letter burned too quickly to give much heat.

8.   The curiously titled book *So You Want to Build a Swamp Basic Sewage Construction Made Simple* lay open before her snoring husband.

9.   While the difficulties were abundantly clear one thing was abundantly murky their solution.

10. The text for last Sunday's sermon was Genesis 28 11 which says "Behold, Esau my brother is a hairy man, and I am a smooth man."

11. David had finally sold all his cars the Volkswagen the Triumph the Fiat and the Toyota.

12. In order to raise capital for the business they had to part with most of the things they had scrimped for the horses even Buddy's colt Tom's pride and joy his sailboat not only the horse trailer and the boat trailer but also the camping trailer they used for hunting season and trips to the beach and everything else that they could get a sum of money out of large or small.

Sentences 13–17 following will test your ability at using *dashes.* The remaining sentences will provide a general review of all the punctuation skills you have studied to this point.

Supply dashes for the following:

13. Dorothy was told to follow the Yellow Brick Road to the Emerald City a name that conjured up visions of green jewels and wealth beyond belief where she was to ask for help from the Wizard of Oz.

14. She hoped to get his aid in returning to Kansas, but she also wanted him to help her companions the Cowardly Lion, the Tin Woodsman, and the Scarecrow to achieve their wishes as well.

15. To gain the Wizard's aid they had to bring him the broomstick of the Wicked Witch of the West the wickedest witch in the history of Oz before he would even listen seriously to their wishes.

16. Getting into the Witch's castle was not too difficult for Dorothy's loyal companions, but getting out alive that's what worried the Scarecrow would be much trickier.

17. Splashing the Witch with water a lucky accident if there ever was one saved them all from deaths too horrible to think about.

Supply punctuation for the following review sentences:

18. Jimmy Hoffa the former Teamster leader disappeared under highly suspicious circumstances.

19. Just before his term of office expired the President made three Supreme Court appointments an action everyone had been long awaiting.

20. The fact of the appointments was not surprising but totally astonishing was the final appointee's political backing the Nazi party.

21. At 10 15 A.M. the launch countdown was scheduled to begin at 10 37 A.M. lift-off was supposed to occur.

22. The San Diego Zoo's collection of baby animals includes three fascinating little creatures playing together in the same enclosure a baby orangutan a baby chimpanzee and a baby gorilla.

23. Three other animals the gigantic Galapagos tortoise the elephant and the rhinoceros share an open-air section surrounded by a concrete ditch too steep to climb and too wide to jump.

24. "When the tour buses arrive" the attendant said "watch the bears sit up and beg for the bread they know will be thrown to them."

25. Three famous tourist attractions in London the Changing of the Guard at Buckingham Palace the British Museum and the Tower of London should not be avoided just because they're tourist attractions.

26. They are after all famous attractions because they've given so many people so much pleasure.

27. This model comes factory-equipped with automatic transmission standard transmission or five-speed racing gears.

28. The prices for the optional equipment were God knows way out of line.

Answers to Self-Test

Compare your answers to the Self-Test to those given below. If you answered all questions correctly, go on to the next chapter. If you missed any, review the frames indicated in parentheses following the answers. If you missed several questions, you should probably look back over the whole chapter before going on.

1. When leaving the aircraft, check that you have the following items ready: your passport, your health certificate (if travelling from certain areas which the steward will announce), your baggage claim tickets, and your boarding pass. (frames 1, 5)

2. Although he might have bought much more duty-free merchandise and still have been within the legal limits, Henry made only three purchases: a bottle of Scotch for his brother, a commemorative china plate for his mother, and a hand-knit cashmere tam for his little sister, Baby June. (frame 6)

3. As he waited in the terminal for the 12:05 flight to arrive, the words of the 23rd Psalm kept going through his mind. (frame 10)

4. Before going on to show how Hamlet's advice to the actors fits in with the rest of the play, I'd like to remind you of what he said:

Speak the speech, I pray you, as I pronounced it to you, trippingly on the tongue. But if you mouth it, as many of your players do, I'd as lief the town crier spoke my lines.

Obviously, maybe too obviously, these words are as appropriate today as when Shakespeare, who was an experienced actor himself, wrote them for his own fellow-actors to hear.   (frame 7)

5. Nobody seemed to notice that he'd forgotten his prepared speech, or maybe nobody cared. At least it worried one person: himself.   (frame 8)

6. Alice wondered why her brothers had always made changing a tire such a big deal when it was such a simple process: jack up the car, take off the flat, put on the spare, and let the car down again. But then the traffic started getting heavier and coming closer and closer, the rain began freezing as it hit the car, and darkness fell faster than she could remember its ever doing before.   (frame 6)

7. When he woke from his daydream, Bob Cratchit found he had written the following:

Dear Mr. Scrooge:

I used up all the coal in trying to keep warm, and then I burned the ledgers. There's only this last scrap of paper left, but there are three remaining pieces of furniture: my stool, this desk, and the bookcase. When they're gone, I go.
Hoping you have a very Merry Christmas I am

The unfinished letter burned too quickly to give much heat.   (frames 1, 7)

8. The curiously titled book, *So You Want to Build a Swamp: Basic Sewage Construction Made Simple,* lay open before her snoring husband.   (frame 1)

9. While the difficulties were abundantly clear, one thing was abundantly murky: their solution.   (frame 8)

10. The text for last Sunday's sermon was Genesis 28:11, which says "Behold, Esau my brother is a hairy man, and I am a smooth man." (frame 1)

11. David had finally sold all his cars: the Volkswagen, the Triumph, the Fiat, and the Toyota.   (frame 6)

12. In order to raise capital for the business, they had to part with most of the things they had scrimped for: the horses, even Buddy's colt; Tom's pride and joy, his sailboat; not only the horse trailer and the boat trailer, but also the camping trailer they used for hunting season and

trips to the beach; and everything else they could get a sum of money out of, large or small. (frame 6)

13. Dorothy was told to follow the Yellow Brick Road to the Emerald City—a name that conjured up visions of green jewels and wealth beyond belief—where she was to ask for help from the Wizard of Oz. (frames 16–18)

14. She hoped to get his aid in returning to Kansas, but she also wanted him to help her companions—the Cowardly Lion, the Tin Woodsman, and the Scarecrow—to achieve their wishes as well. (frames 12–15)

15. To gain the Wizard's aid they had to bring him the broomstick of the Wicked Witch of the West—the wickedest witch in the history of Oz— before he would even listen seriously to their wishes. (frames 16–18)

16. Getting into the Witch's castle was not too difficult for Dorothy's loyal companions, but getting out alive—that's what worried the Scarecrow—would be much trickier. (frames 16–17)

17. Splashing the Witch with water—a lucky accident if ever there was one— saved them all from deaths too horrible to think about. (frames 16–18)

18. Jimmy Hoffa, the former Teamster leader, disappeared under highly suspicious circumstances. (Chapter 3, frame 27)

19. Just before his term of office expired, the President made three Supreme Court appointments: an action everyone had been long awaiting. (Chapter 3, frame 26; this chapter, frame 8)

20. The fact of the appointments was not surprising, but totally astonishing was the final appointee's political backing: the Nazi party. (Chapter 3, frame 1; this chapter, frame 8)

21. At 10:15 A.M. the launch countdown was scheduled to begin; at 10:37 A.M. lift-off was supposed to occur. (Chapter 4, frames 5 and 15; this chapter, frame 11)

22. The San Diego Zoo's collection of baby animals includes three fascinating little creatures playing together in the same enclosure: a baby orangutan, a baby chimpanzee, and a baby gorilla. (this chapter, frame 6)

23. Three other animals—the gigantic Galapagos tortoise, the elephant, and the rhinoceros—share an open-air section surrounded by a concrete ditch too steep to climb and too wide to jump. (this chapter, frames 12–15)

24. "When the tour buses arrive," the attendant said, "watch the bears sit up and beg for the bread they know will be thrown to them." (Chapter 3, frame 17c)

25. Three famous tourist attractions in London—the Changing of the Guard at Buckingham Palace, the British Museum, and the Tower of London—should not be avoided just because they're tourist attractions. (this chapter, frames 12-15)

26. They are, after all, famous attractions because they've given so many people so much pleasure. (Chapter 3, frame 17c)

27. This model comes factory-equipped with automatic transmission, standard transmission, or five-speed racing gears. (Chapter 3, frame 3)

28. The prices for the optional equipment were—God knows—way out of line. (this chapter, frames 16-18)

CHAPTER SIX

Parentheses, Brackets, Italics, and the Slash

In this chapter we will cover punctuation marks that in one way or another set off material within a sentence, or set off words or items on a page.

Parentheses and brackets are similar in function: each is designed to set off material that relates to the content of the sentence but that is distinctly separate from the structure of the sentence itself.

In print, italics, a type style with characters that slant upward to the right, are used to show that something is more important or very different from the rest of the words on the page. In handwritten or typed material, you use underlining to show italics. If your writing goes to a printer, then the underlined words are actually set into italic type. Since italicizing a word is, short of setting the word in all capital letters or another type-face altogether, the strongest emphasis you can give, obviously your use of underlining should be restrained. *REMEMBER, YOU CAN'T EMPHASIZE EVERY-THING!* (See what I mean?)

The slash serves in a variety of fields, ranging from poetry to mathematics. Its main use is in separating items to maintain clarity and avoid confusion.

OBJECTIVES

When you have completed this chapter, you should be able to:

- use parentheses in numbering a list;
- use parentheses in documentation;
- use parentheses so as to include important content material that does not fit in with the sentence structure;
- use brackets to indicate editorial additions, corrections, or explanations;

- use parentheses to change tone and indicate the writer's attitude;
- use italics as appropriate signals;
- distinguish between the uses of italics and quotation marks;
- use possessive forms with gerunds;
- use the slash mark in dividing words and numerals.

1.   Both parentheses and brackets appear in pairs, as do commas when they enclose parenthetical material, but with this difference: when parenthetical material enclosed by commas occurs at the end of the sentence, the last comma vanishes; the period closes the construction and the entire sentence at once.

I decided, however, to stay.

I decided to stay, however.

2.   Try shifting the material set off by commas in the following and repunctuating the sentences.

(a)   It was impossible, nevertheless, to raise his speed.

(b)   Driver-training classes, no doubt, reduce accidents.

(c)   Dry flies, apparently, are the only lures to use.

— — — — — — — — — — — — — — — —

(a)   It was impossible to raise his speed, nevertheless.
(b)   Driver-training classes reduce accidents, no doubt.
(c)   Dry flies are the only lures to use, apparently.

3.   As you can see, the second comma disappears. But when you use parentheses or brackets, the second mark remains:

In the Beginnings, published in 1963, is rather different in tone from *From Ape to Angel* (1958).

Dry flies are the only lures to use (apparently).

Notice the shift in tone that happens in this last sentence, compared to its uses above in frame 2. When you add the parentheses here, suddenly the sentence is not just a statement of fact, as it appeared to be in frame

2(c). Now it takes on a quality of being not quite true, or at least slightly dubious. We've created a slight shift in meaning by shifting punctuation.

4.   Parentheses are sometimes used (1) to enclose the numerals that number items in a list, (2) to enclose brief documentary references and such items as publishing dates or the dates of a life-span when these would be awkward in written-out form as part of the sentence, and (3) to enclose material that gives essential information but which is impossible to include in the sentence construction.

Apply this third use sparingly. Too frequent use of parentheses makes for choppy sentences. Often you'd be better off to reconstruct the sentence, or to add a sentence, than to crowd in the leftover thoughts parenthetically.

As can be seen by examing the tombs' contents, over hundreds of centuries the artifacts buried with royalty (who in almost all primitive agricultural societies were at least associated with deity if not actually deified themselves) came to be richer and richer in material value and in workmanship, until finally we reach culmination of such development in the tomb of Tut.

5.   Are the patrentheses justifiable in this example? (Yes/No) _____

– – – – – – – – – – – – – – – –

yes

6.   What explanation can you give for their use?

– – – – – – – – – – – – – – – –

The material within parentheses is entirely relevant to the general topic. Yet the topic of this particular sentence, the richness of tomb contents, does not lend itself to including this information easily within the sentence. Made into a separate sentence, it would interrupt the ongoing discussion of tomb holdings. It might be dropped into a footnote, but included as it is in a parenthesis, it gives us useful information without leading us astray from the general point of the discussion.

7.   Now read this passage and decide about its use of the parenthesis. Is it appropriate? (Yes/No) _____

> As John Carson-Smyth, in his essay "On Trivia," says: ". . . gobble-dygook . . . is a word so familiar to us that we seldom take the trouble (and I certainly don't think it's my job) to think about what it means . . ." (page 75).

———————————————

yes and no

8.   Which uses of parenthesis are wrong? Why?

———————————————

The parenthetical insertion within the sentence is wrong. You never put your words into another writer's mouth, and that's what happened in this passage.

9.   If a writer wants to comment on or add to the words he's quoting, the only honest way to do so is by putting his own words in brackets. Brackets are the signal which tells the reader that the writer is adding something not in the original.

10.   Which use of parenthesis in frame 7 is right? Why?

———————————————

The page reference, a brief parenthetical documentation, is right. The page number, not being part of the quoted material, falls outside the final quotation marks. But since it is part of this sentence rather than the one to follow, it falls before the period that closes the sentence.

11.   Now summarize the uses of parentheses as we have observed them. How are parentheses used?

(a)

(b)

(c)

_ _ _ _ _ _ _ _ _ _ _ _ _ _ _

(a) to enclose numerals that number items in a list
(b) to enclose brief documentary references and such items as dates
     when these will not otherwise fit into the sentence
(c) to include essential information that cannot be handled in the
     sentence proper

12. Brackets are a highly specialized mark. They are used (as we noted in
     frame 9 above) to enclose insertions in quoted material, to enclose
     editorial corrections, and occasionally to enclose an editorial explana-
     tion.

> As the felon remarked on his way to the gallows, "I would rather
> be hanged for a sheep then [*sic*] a goat." But it is certain that he
> didn't mean he wanted to be hanged twice, first for a sheep and
> *then* for a goat.

Note: the word [*sic*] in brackets is an editorial insertion. It means that
the word or words preceding it did, in fact, appear exactly as quoted.
It comes from the Latin word *sicut:* "just as," "so as," or "as." *Sic* is
a useful term, because it shows who is responsible for the error in
question.

13. By means of an editorial insertion, supply the name of the author, John
     Milspot, who is being described in this quotation:

> "He found that it was always a struggle for him to hold back his
> sense of humor; it kept popping up even when he had serious matters
> to discuss."

_ _ _ _ _ _ _ _ _ _ _ _ _ _

A possibility: "He [Milspot] found that it was always a struggle for
him to hold back his sense of humor; it kept popping up even when
he had serious matters to discuss."

14.   Here is another example:

"Wood, as a colonel in the army, had studied medicine [actually, law], which he practiced in Oregon after his outraged resignation."

What is the purpose of the brackets here?

_ _ _ _ _ _ _ _ _ _ _ _ _ _ _

To include a correction.

15.   Brackets are used like parentheses *within parentheses*.

The Association of Oil Producing Nations (OPEC) raised international prices for the third time this year, but this action had been anticipated (according to documents of the NAM [National Association of Manufacturers]) in a series of price hikes by the large oil-using companies; these occurred months before the recent OPEC action.

Ernest Hemingway's famous World War I souvenir belt-buckle carried the legend *Gott mit uns* ("God is with us" [which could also be interpreted less nationalistically as "May God be with us"]), and this piece of the flamboyant correspondent's costume must have startled the German prisoners he met during the latter months of World War II.

Note: In technical writing and in many academic fields, this is reversed— that is, brackets enclose parentheses. When you prepare material for a specialized field, you should, of course, follow the preferred style for that field.

16.   In formal writing, underlining should be avoided except where showing stress is crucial. In personal or informal situations, like letters to friends or where the whole tone of the piece is more emphatic than usual, perhaps greater use of italics would be useful and even to be expected. But these are exceptions.

There are some places in formal writing where italics (underlining) are regularly used and expected. One of these cases, the underlining of book titles, you have already seen. Besides the titles of books, can you think of anything else that is regularly italicized?

_ _ _ _ _ _ _ _ _ _ _ _ _ _ _

In general, the titles of *whole* published works: hence, the titles of poems published as separate works, the titles of plays; the names of ships, works of art, movies, and foreign words and phrases also are italicized.

17. Parts of a published work—chapters, individual poems, short stories, stories or articles in periodicals—are shown by quotation marks. *Whole* works are shown by italics. Again, punctuation is a signal of meaning.

18. Punctuate the following sentences.

   (a)   Dr. and Mrs. J. Q. Firestone sailed on the Lusitania's maiden voyage

   (b)   We read about it in The Talk of the Town in The New Yorker

   (c)   "Have you read the story I think it was in Galaxy about peoples stray paper clips turning into coat hangers" Sam asked

   (d)   "The pro-busing group has had its problems" a spokesperson reported today "But" he added "we have every reason to be confident"

   (e)   "Everyone has a rose" the supervisor reported "and every rose has its tag"

   (f)   Did he say "Class is cancelled Monday"

   (g)   After talking it over we decided to support the following causes UNESCO UNICEF and UGN

- - - - - - - - - - - - - - - -

   (a)   Dr. and Mrs. J. Q. Firestone sailed on the Lusitania's maiden voyage.
   (b)   We read about it in "The Talk of the Town" in The New Yorker.
   (c)   "Have you read the story—I think it was in Galaxy—about people's stray paper clips' turning into coat hangers?" Sam asked.
   (d)   "The pro-busing group has had its problems," a spokesperson reported today. "But," he added, "we have every reason to be confident."
   (e)   "Everyone has a rose," the supervisor reported, "and every rose has its tag."

(f)   Did he say "Class is cancelled Monday"?

(g)   After talking it over, we decided to support the following causes: UNESCO, UNICEF, and UGN.

19.   Sentence (c) illustrates a special use of the possessive case. The word *turning* is a gerund; that is, it's a verb ending in *-ing* used as a noun. When this occurs, the word that is really the subject, or doer, of the gerund's action takes the possessive form. Here are some other gerunds:

Running was his favorite pastime.

We liked *leaving* early.

Skipping and *hopping* are forms of *jumping.*

A noun or a pronoun governing a gerund takes the possessive form.

His leaving so abruptly worried us.

The conveyor *belt's* breaking was the cause of the trouble.

George's drinking was excessive.

The *ship's* sailing caused *Juliet's* weeping.

In all these cases, as you can see, the possessive form follows logic: the gerund "belongs to" the word that takes the possessive form—the sailing of the ship, the weeping of Juliet, the drinking of George, etc.

Convert the parenthetical material in the following sentences into gerund phrases with possessives:

(a)   In the play, *Twelfth Night,* (the smiling of Malvolio) is calculated to make Countess Olivia ill.

(b)   (the laughing of us) made them irritated.

(c)   (the planning of the skipper) to sail on the ebb was known to the crew.

(d)   The problem of (the running hot of the motor) was not expected from (the testing of the engineers).

_ _ _ _ _ _ _ _ _ _ _ _ _ _ _

(a) Malvolio's smiling;   (b) Our laughing;   (c) The skipper's planning;
(d) the motor's running hot, the engineers' testing

20. The slash (/) has a variety of functions. It is used to separate numbers as in fractions and dates: 12/29/72; 1/5; 5/12; 15/37. It is used to show alternatives: either/or, true/false, yes/no, and/or. It is used to show the end of a line of poetry, when you are quoting it within your text, instead of quoting it in a block of verse; two lines of poetry should be set in quotation marks and separated by a slash, as in:

> Among my favorite limericks is one beginning: "There was a young man from Nantucket / Who was fishing for whales in a bucket."

> Unlike the view he gives us in the foolish lovers of his plays, Shakespeare's ideal of love can be found in these lines from Sonnet 116: "Let me not to the marriage of true minds / Admit impediments."

SELF-TEST

This Self-Test will help you determine how well you have met the objectives for this chapter and whether you are ready to go on to the next chapter. The answers to this Self-Test follow.

Supply or correct the punctuation in the sentences below.

1. As the famous critic, Edmund Allan Leanfellow, was fond of remarking, "If Huckleberry Finn isn't at least partly autobiographical, then his Twain's boyhood was duller than I'd guess from reading that book."

2. *"Charlie's sic Aunt"* notes a misspelling; it is not the same as saying the play, Charley's Aunt, is sick, despite the fact that the main character is in drag.

3. "For safety's sake," the sergeant bellowed, "it is absolutely necessary to follow these directions in exactly the following order: (1) pull out pin, (2) throw grenade, (3) drop to ground. Last platoon through here, some jerk pulled the pin, dropped to the ground, and *then* tried to throw it from a prune (sic) position!"

4. In his Bands of Americans, Edgar Glockenspiel writes: "At the turn of the century lived John Philip Sousa, 1854–1932, the Waltz (actually, March) King (p. 95)."

5. The first two lines of Lewis Carroll's poem "Jabberwock" are " 'Twas brillig, and the slithy toves Did gyre and gimble in the wabe."

6. "The major cause of the War of 1812 1812–15 is often described as the impression sic of American sailors on the high seas."

7. The solar eclipse will reach totality at 637 A.M. Pacific Standard Time 937 A.M. Eastern Standard Time.

8. Although Sousa is given credit some might say blame for the invention of the sousaphone he only suggested its development, others designed and built it.

9. Objective tests usually involve true-false questions and-or multiple-choice questions.

10. July 4, 1776, is much more stirring to the patriot than when the date is reduced to the numbers 7-4-76; it is also less confusing.

Answers to Self-Test

Compare your answers on the Self-Test to those given below. If you answered all questions correctly, go on to the next chapter. If you missed any, review the frames indicated in parentheses following the answers. If you missed several questions, you should probably look back over the whole chapter before going on.

1. As the famous critic, Edmund Allan Leanfellow was fond of remarking, "If Huckleberry Finn isn't at least partly autobiographical, then his [Twain's] boyhood was duller than I'd guess from reading that book." (frames 13, 16, 17)

2. "*Charlie's* [*sic*] *Aunt*" notes a misspelling; it is not the same as saying the play, Charley's Aunt, is sick, despite the fact that the main character is in drag. (frames 12, 16, 17)

3. "For safety's sake," the sergeant bellowed, "it is absolutely necessary to follow these directions in exactly the following order: (1) pull out pin, (2) throw grenade, (3) drop to ground. Last platoon through here, some jerk pulled the pin, dropped to the ground, and *then* tried to throw it from a prune [sic] position!" (frames 4, 12)

4. In his Bands of Americans, Edgar Glockenspiel writes: "At the turn of the century lived John Philip Sousa (1854-1932), the Waltz [actually, March] King" (p. 95). (frames 3, 4, 14, 16, 17)

5. The first two lines of Lewis Carroll's poem "Jabberwock" are " 'Twas brillig, and the slithy toves / Did gyre and gimble in the wabe." (frames 17, 18, 20)

6. "The major cause of the War of 1812 (1812–15) is often described as the impression [sic] of American sailors on the high seas." (frames 3, 4, 12)

7. The solar eclipse will reach totality at 6:37 A.M. Pacific Standard Time (9:37 A.M. Eastern Standard Time). (frame 4)

8. Although Sousa is given credit (Some might say blame.) for the invention of the sousaphone, he only suggested its development; others designed and built it. (frame 4)

9. Objective tests usually involve true/false questions and/or multiple choice questions. (frame 20)

10. July 4, 1776, is much more stirring to the patriot than when the date is reduced to the numbers 7/4/76; it is also less confusing. (frame 20)

CHAPTER SEVEN

Abbreviations and Hyphens

Some useful punctuation marks have nothing whatever to do with sentence structure but deal, instead, with relationships between individual words or parts of words, or indicate missing parts of words. The abbreviation period and the hyphen are such marks. In this chapter we will cover both.

The abbreviation period indicates the end of a word that has been shortened; it saves writing space and reading time for words so frequently used that there's little chance of confusing them, even when they're no longer all there. It doesn't indicate the end of a sentence.

While the hyphen might seem to be the most insignificant of punctuation marks, it sometimes carries the whole weight of the sentence's meaning. Consider the difference in the meanings of the following sentence pairs:

(a) A squad of six foot-soldiers manned the bunker.
(b) A squad of six-foot soldiers manned the bunker.

(a) To avoid eye-fatigue, and thus errors, they each took three quarter-hour shifts at the radar screen.
(b) To avoid eye-fatigue, and thus errors, they each took three-quarter-hour shifts at the radar screen.

Obviously, the meaning changes drastically with the movement of the hyphen.

Hyphens have the function of either joining or separating words or parts of words. But whichever the hyphen is used for, clarity of meaning is its purpose.

Like abbreviations, hyphenated words are subject to changes in accepted usage, so in most cases an up-to-date dictionary is your only protection against errors. Still, certain general statements can be made.

OBJECTIVES

When you have completed this chapter, you should be able to:

- use the most common abbreviations without error;
- avoid errors in abbreviation duplication;
- use common Latin abbreviations or their English equivalents;
- use abbreviations of printing references;
- use hyphens correctly to form compound adjectives;
- recognize and use standard compound nouns that are hyphenated;
- recognize the need for using a dictionary to identify words compounded without hyphens;
- use the hyphen for clarity's sake;
- identify and solve basic syllabication problems.

1.   Abbreviations other than Mr., Mrs., Dr., A.M., P.M., A.D., and B.C. are usually avoided in formal, nontechnical writing.
      When using these common abbreviations, the writer must observe the customs that go along with them:

   (a)   These abbreviations are always accompanied by the appropriate surname, date, or numeral. (Exception: St. for Saint takes the first name, as in St. Joan, St. Michael, etc.) They may not be used alone. Thus we have:

>   She went to see Dr. Stoat.
>   She went to see the Dr. (Unacceptable)

>   Mrs. Jones is our neighbor
>   Jones, our neighbor, is a Mrs. (Unacceptable)

>   Aristophanes wrote his comedies about 400 B.C.
>   Aristophanes wrote his comedies B.C.

>   The meeting was to have taken place after noon.
>   *Or:* The meeting was to have taken place at about 3:30 P.M.
>   The meeting was to have taken place P.M. (Unacceptable)

   (b)   Some abbreviations always *follow* names, such as: Jr., Sr., B.A., Ph.D., LL.D., M.D., D.D.S., Esq. However, they are never used *after* a name when you have used a similar title before the name. For instance:

>   I made out the check to my dentist, John Periodontia, D.M.D., and mailed it yesterday afternoon.

Or:

I made out the check to my dentist, Dr. John Periodontia, and mailed it yesterday afternoon.

Not: I made out the check to my dentist, Dr. John Periodontia, D.M.D., and mailed it yesterday afternoon.

Not: Dr. Fred Femur, M.D.; Dr. Lon Learned, Ph.D.; Mr. George Knight, Esq.; Dr. W. Cuspid, D.D.S.

Correct the abbreviations used in the following:

(a)   I wasted too much time the other day waiting for the P.M. train.

(b)   The famous immunologist, Dr. Jonas Salk, was to speak to the medical faculty last week.

(c)   Dr. Henry Kissinger, Ph.D., had travelled thousands of airmiles in attempting to bring those nations together.

(d)   He went to see the Dr. this A.M.

(e)   They visited the shrine of St. Assisi.

(a)   I wasted too much time the other day waiting for the afternoon train. (or 4:15 P.M., or other specified time)

(b)   no correction needed

(c)   Dr. Henry Kissinger *or* Henry Kissinger, Ph.D.

(d)   He went to see the doctor this morning.

(e)   They visited the shrine of St. Francis. (*or* St. Francis of Assisi)

2.   Many Latin abbreviations are still in common use in very formal writing situations—in learned journals and books, for instance. But in less formal writing, such abbreviations—*i.e.* for "that is," *e.g.* for "for example," *etc.* for "and so forth"—are increasingly giving way to their English equivalents which are short and clear.

In the following sentences, try replacing the Latin with English expressions:

(a)   Some English professors are excessively fond of sesquipedalian obfuscation, i.e., they are in love with the bewildering effect of long words.

(b)   Words meaning the young of a species— colts, lambs, calves, etc.— are usually words having good connotations, e.g., "He's a perfect lamb," or "She's a regular kitten."

(c)   Another sort of connotation is given by "He's a perfect sheep,"
"She's a regular cat," etc.

(a) that is;   (b) and so forth, for example;   (c) and so forth.

3.   The above abbreviations call for the use of periods. Some abbreviations,
however, do not. Our daily language diet is filled with "alphabet soup"
composed of the initials of various organizations, many of them more
familiar as abbreviations than as spelled-out names: UNESCO, NASA,
AIM, ARCO, NATO, OPEC, UNICEF, CETA, SAC, SAT, SALT, etc.
But when do you abbreviate such things *with* and when *without* periods?
Only your dictionary—and it must be a *recent* dictionary—can tell you.
Forty years ago, the FBI was the F.B.I.

4.   In technical writing, which usually involves matters of quantity, abbreviations commonly occur after numbers. These are to be found in such
various places as cookbooks, traffic regulations, and physics texts. Some
examples:

1/4 tsp. salt; 32°F; 680 mph; 700 cfm; 750 rpm; 5 ft. 10 in.; 3 m
6 cm; 500 cc; 100°C.

Again, unless such abbreviations are very familiar to you, you should
check a dictionary to be sure which require periods.

5.   Some words are spelled out in the body of a piece of writing but are
abbreviated when they appear in parenthetical references or in notes.
For example:

page (p.), pages (pp.), volume (vol.), lines 340 to 352 (ll. 340–52),
Chapter Five (ch. 5).

6.   The hyphen is used to join two words that form a compound adjective
used *before* the noun. Here are some examples:

The gray-green German uniform was called *Feldgrau*.
But: *Feldgrau*, the German uniform color, was gray green.

The slow-moving runner was caught at first base.
But: The runner caught at first base was slow moving.

Corn-fed cattle bring the best prices.

But: Cattle bringing the best prices are corn fed.

Exceptions:

When the adjective is preceded by an adverb, no hyphen is used—no compound is formed. For instance:

The slowly moving runner was caught at first base.

Totally corn-fed cattle bring even better prices.

7.   Hyphens are used in certain standard compound words, such as: (father, son, brother, mother, daughter, sister·)-in-law; great-grand(mother, father, etc.); step-(son, daughter, mother, etc.), A-bomb, and X-ray.

The words involving family relationships seem to have been "frozen" in their hyphenated forms. But most compounds develop through certain phases, from adjective + noun, to adjective-hyphen-noun, to adjectivenoun. For example: (early form) police man, (middle form) policeman, (final form) policeman. Without a current dictionary, most of us are not sure how far a word has progressed toward accepted fusion of adjective and noun. As it is gradually accepted, no doubt we will soon be spelling X-ray: Xray, then xray.

Try using the hyphen in the following:

(a)   His great granddaughter, a three foot midget, had married a ten foot side show giant and had found a career in show business.

(b)   A six inch trout is a legal catch, but this one only measures five inches.

(c)   A bomb blasts are measured in megatons; the recent test was a fifty megaton explosion.

(d)   Besides neutron and X ray radiation, high velocity gamma particles are dangerous factors in atomic tests.

(e)   The post office location was convenient for rail and bus traffic, but it lacked off street parking for the postmen who worked there.

— — — — — — — — — — — — —

(a)   His great-granddaughter, a three-foot midget, had married a ten-foot side-show giant and had found a career in show business.

(b) A six-inch trout is a legal catch, but this one only measures five inches.

(c) A-bomb blasts are measured in megatons; the recent test was a fifty-megaton explosion.

(d) Besides neutron and X-ray radiation, high-velocity gamma particles are dangerous factors in atomic tests.

(e) The post-office location was convenient for rail and bus traffic, but it lacked off-street parking for the postmen who worked there.

8.   English, like all living languages, continues to grow and change. One means of growth is the creation of new words by combining, as we saw in the case of the word *policeman* in the last frame. Another way is by the addition of prefixes (like *ex-, semi-, pre-, pro-*) and suffixes (like *-like, -elect*). Where they are not yet absorbed into one word, or where they need to be kept separated by a hyphen for the sake of clarity, the hyphen is used. For instance, when adding a prefix causes a doubling of letters (re-entry, pre-election) the hyphen avoids confusion. Or when the meaning may be distorted (After the police recovered his stolen convertible, he had to re-cover the top.), the hyphen serves to clarify.

     Try these sentences:

(a) The semi literate bookkeeper's semiweekly reports were audited semiannually.

(b) Reports from exPresident Nixon's doctors state that the tumor like mass they removed was benign.

(c) The committee had worked hard to reelect him, and the governor elect, an exlawyer, gave them his promise to reform the judicial system, even if it meant reforming the defunct Task Force on Criminal Justice.

(d) Generally speaking, Governor-Elect Smith is honest.

--- --- --- --- --- --- --- --- --- ---

(a) The semi-literate bookkeeper's semiweekly reports were audited semiannually. ("Semiweekly" and "semiannually" are examples of the absorbed prefix, according to my dictionary.)

(b) Reports from ex-President Nixon's doctors state that the tumor-like mass they removed was benign. (The prefix *ex-* is not capitalized even when used in titles that form part of a name.)

(c) The committee had worked hard to re-elect him, and the governor-elect, an ex-lawyer, gave them his promise to reform the judicial system, even if it meant re-forming the defunct Task Force on Criminal Justice.

(d) Generally speaking, Governor-elect Smith is honest. (As with *ex-* in (b) above, the suffix *-elect* is not capitalized even though it seems part of the name.)

9. Almost every time you write a check, you observe the next use of hyphenation. Hyphens are used to separate all written-out numbers from twenty-one to ninety-nine and to separate the parts of written-out fractions, such as: one-fourth, two and one-half, three and three-fourths, etc.

Convert the following numerals into words:

(a) 243

(b) 12 1/3

(c) 6.3

_ _ _ _ _ _ _ _ _ _ _ _ _ _ _

(a) two hundred forty-three; (b) twelve and one-third; (c) six and three-tenths

10. In practicing the next use of the hyphen, you will nearly always need the help of a dictionary. The term for it is *syllabication*, a fairly self-explanatory word. It means the use of a hyphen between syllables when a word must be divided at the end of a line.

Some basic rules:

(1) A single-syllable word may *never* be divided (examples: tough, smooth, width, through).

(2) Two letters that make a single sound may not be separated (examples: *th* as in *either, sh* as in *smashing, ai* as in *brainpower, ck* as in *luckily*).

(3) Divide the word after the prefix or before the suffix, unless this alters the pronunciation (examples: pre-natal, anti-disestablishmentarian, dis-place, displace-ment, corpora-tion, dis-regard, disregard-ing).

(4)   Divide the word after a vowel; again, you may not alter pronunciation (examples: intensi-fied, demonstra-tor, ana-lyze, indecent).

(5)   Do not divide off fewer than three letters at the end of a line.

Using the above rules, check for errors in the following divided words:

(a) modifi-er; (b) examina-tion; (c) ex-iting (d) dis-hcloth;

(e) dis-close; (f) pluc-kily; (g) small-est; (h) umbili-cal;

(i) smo-othe; (j) o-mit

_ _ _ _ _ _ _ _ _ _ _ _ _ _ _ _

(a) incorrect—see (5); (b) correct; (c) incorrect—see (5);
(d) incorrect—see (2); (e) correct; (f) incorrect—see (2);
(g) correct; (h) correct; (i) incorrect—see (1) (j) incorrect—see (5).

Time now to check your ability in using the abbreviation and the hyphen.

SELF-TEST

This Self-Test will help you determine how well you have met the objectives for this chapter and whether you are ready to go on to the next chapter. The answers to this Self-Test follow.

Correct any abbreviation errors in the following sentences:

1. Einstein's most famous concept, ie, the theory of general relativity, will be the subject of this P.M.'s lecture.

2. Mr and Mrs Alfred Doolittle will be the guests of honor at the club's breakfast meeting tomorrow A.M.

3. We walked three blocks down the St. to look at the statue of the St. of Arc.

4. While I'm sure Dr. Smith, Jr., is a fine doctor, I feel more comfortable with Dr. Smith, Sr.

5. Dr. Jewel Feldspar, Ph.D., is the senior member of the geology faculty.

6. The formula called for raising the solution temperature to 550°Cent. and centrifuging it slowly at no more than 55 R.P.M.

7. A week later, one A.M. he was driving to work along Green St. and saw Harry Smith's Mrs.

8. The statements on the previous three pp. have no relationship to the charts on page 368, which are also mistakenly reproduced in ch. 4.

Punctuate the following, where necessary.

9.   proJohnson
10. scrolllike
11. exwife
12. a well known man
13. a man, well known for . . .

14. twentytwo and threefourths
15. molelike
16. fireeating
17. semiprofessional

Which of the following words may be divided at the end of a line?

18. through
19. thorough

20. common

21. compound

22. and

23. obey

24. ploughed

25. malignant

26. erupt

27. harpy

28. drain

Answers to Self-Test

Compare your answers to the Self-Test to those given below. If you answered all questions correctly, go on to the next chapter. If you missed any, review the frames indicated in parentheses following the answers. If you missed several questions, you should probably look back over the whole chapter before going on.

1.   i.e.,; this afternoon's lecture   (frames 2, 1)

2.   Mr. and Mrs.; tomorrow morning   (frame 1)

3.   down the street; St. Joan (*or* St. Joan of Arc)   (frame 1)

4.   no corrections needed (Jr. and Sr. are not the same as Dr.—M.D. would have been unnecessary here.)   (frame 1b)

5.   drop either Dr. or Ph.D.   (frame 1b)

6. $550°C$; 55 rpm (or r.p.m.)   (frame 4)

7.   one morning; Green Street; Mrs. Harry Smith (*or* Harry Smith's wife)   (frame 1)

8.   previous three pages; the fourth chapter (*or* Chapter Four)   (frame 5)

9.   pro-Johnson   (frame 8)

10. scroll-like   (frame 8)

11. ex-wife   (frame 8)

12. a well-known man   (frame 6)

13. correct   (frame 6)

14. twenty-two and three-fourths   (frame 9)

15. correct   (frame 8)

16. fire-eating   (frame 8)

17. semi-professional   (frame 8)

18. no   (frame 10)
19. yes (frame 10)
20. yes (frame 10)
21. yes (frame 10)
22. no   (frame 10)
23. no   (frame 10)
24. no   (frame 10)
25. yes (frame 10)
26. no   (frame 10)
27. no   (frame 10)
28. no   (frame 10)

CHAPTER EIGHT

The Apostrophe and Quotation Marks

In this chapter we will cover two punctuation marks that are very alike in appearance but are very different in meaning: the apostrophe (') and quotation marks (" ' "').

Apostrophes have three main uses: (1) to show possession, (2) to show omission of letters or numbers in contractions, and (3) with an added s, to show the plural of numerals, of letters, and of words used as units. Some examples will help clarify these:

(1) *Possession:* child's, children's, mother-in-law's, dog's, dogs', George's, someone else's

(2) *Omission:* can't (for *cannot*), shan't (for *shall not*), haven't (for *have not*), '99 (for *1899*), o'clock (for *of the clock*)

(3) *Plurals:*   You forgot to add the *10*'s.
You make your *Q*'s oddly.
But me no *but*'s!

Like other types of punctuation, the apostrophe serves to convey meaning. In the above examples, it shows the following: who's the possessor, where there's an omission, and when there's more than one of a thing.

The other punctuation marks that are not related to sentence structure are quotation marks, used whenever you work with other people's words, to show direct speech or words taken exactly from someone else's writing.

OBJECTIVES

When you have completed this chapter, you should be able to:

- use apostrophes to show possession;
- use apostrophes to show omissions or contractions;

- use apostrophes to indicate plurals;
- use quotation marks to indicate direct quotations;
- recognize when quotation marks are not needed, as in indirect quotations;
- use quotation marks to designate titles of short pieces of writing;
- use quotation marks to cite unusual words or words used in unusual senses.

1. Here are some rules of thumb for using the apostrophe to show possession.

    (a)   Add an apostrophe plus an *s* to words not ending in *s:*

        Examples: men's, Sam's, people's, ship's

    (b)   If the word is *singular* and ends in *s*, do the same, *unless this makes the word hard to say.*

        Examples: jackass's stubbornness; harness's strength; grass's greenness; miss's dress; Thomas's doubt; Boas's scholarship

        Not Mercedes's, but Mercedes' styling; not Wiggins's, but Wiggins' cabbage patch; not Aristophanes's, but Aristophanes' comedies.

    (c)   If the word is *plural* and ends in *s*, add only the apostrophe.

        Examples: horses' stables, ships' berths, dragoons' barracks, girls' locker room

In the following, test your understanding of the possessive apostrophe by converting the parenthetical material into a possessive plus noun. For example:

The (hats belonging to the ladies) were gorgeous.
The ladies' hats were gorgeous.

(a)   All the (blankets belonging to the girls) were pink.

(b)   One (hat of a lady) was new, but the other (hats of ladies) were not.

(c)   (hats for men) were on sale.

(d)   All of (the works of Heraclitus) are lost.

(e)   The (blankets of the children) are in the laundry.

(f)   (the codes of one society) may differ from (those of another).

(g)   (men of Xerxes) were powerful and soldierly.

(h)   The (stables of the cavalry horses) were ancient.

(i)   (governors of twenty states) attended the conference.

_ _ _ _ _ _ _ _ _ _ _ _ _ _ _ _

(a)   All the girls' blankets were pink.
(b)   One lady's hat was new, but the other ladies' hats were not.
(c)   Men's hats were on sale.
(d)   All of Heraclitus' works are lost.
(e)   The children's blankets are in the laundry.
(f)   One society's codes may differ from another's.
(g)   Xerxes' men were powerful and soldierly.
(h)   The cavalry horses' stables were ancient.
(i)   Twenty states' governors attended the conference.

2.   There are two situations in using the apostrophe to show possession
     that seem, at first glance, to be tricky. Actually, they're quite reasonable
     and are connected with the meaning you want to show. One is the pos-
     sessive compound. In these, simply attach the apostrophe + s to the
     last word:

> great-grandfather's pipe
> both mothers-in-law's corsages
> no one else's business

The other situation involves joint possession. Here, too, the apostrophe + s attaches to the last word. In cases of *individual* possession,
each word naturally is possessive—this keeps the meaning clear. For
instance:

> Groucho, Chico, and Harpo's act (joint)
> Groucho's, Chico's, and Harpo's girls were each absolute beauties.
> (individual)

> Mary and Martha's father (joint)
> Mary's and Martha's husbands (individual)

Supply the possessive signals necessary for the following in making
the parenthetical word or words possessive:

(a)   (Jane and Harry) brother

    (b)   (someone else) car

    (c)   (daughter-in-law) (ex-husband) alimony

    (d)   (great-grandsons) education

    (e)   (Tom, Dick, and Mary) Bar and Grill

— — — — — — — — — — — — — — —

    (a)   Jane and Harry's brother
    (b)   someone else's car
    (c)   daughter-in-law's ex-husband's alimony
    (d)   great-grandsons' education *or* great-grandson's education, depending on meaning
    (e)   Tom, Dick, and Mary's Bar and Grill

3.   Apostrophes also show omissions of letters or numbers. These may occur in everyday abbreviations, like *can't* or *won't,* or they may show that regularly pronounced sounds are being omitted, as in reproducing dialects. For example:

> "Sure an' if I'd known yez wuz boozin' down t' O'Flaherty's since six o'clock I'd not ha' bin worryin' myself sicker'n me Ma was in the Troubles o' the '20's."

This may be bad "stage Irish," but it contains several of the apostrophe uses described above. Write out in full the words in which omissions occur:

— — — — — — — — — — — — — — —

> "Sure, *and* if *I had* known yez was *boozing* down *to* O'Flaherty's since six *of the clock I would* not *have* bin *worrying* myself *sicker than* me Ma was in the Troubles of the *1920's.*"

4.   The final major use of the apostrophe is to show that you're using a letter, numeral, or word in the plural. As with the possessive, you form this by adding the apostrophe plus *s* to the word; one more signal is added: you italicize (underline) the letter, number, or word so treated, but you do *not* italicize the *s.* Here are some examples:

Hide your eyes and count to 300 by 5's.

How many s's are in "possessive"?

There are too many *and*'s and *but*'s in this paragraph.

Cautions:

(a)   This is the *only* situation in which you use the apostrophe to form the plural.

(b)   The apostrophe is never used with possessive pronouns, like *his, hers, its, whose, theirs, ours, yours.* (It's always means it is; who's always means who is.)

(c)   The apostrophe is never used to form the plural of proper names. ("There are three Georges in class." *Not:* "There are three George's in class." *But:* "This George's the best-looking of the three Georges." Here, "George's" means "George is"—it's a contraction, not a possessive. *But:* "George's dollar flew over the Potomac."—possessive: it's his dollar.)

5.   This sentence illustrates the use of quotation marks:

"John, I've lost my identification bracelet," Octavia said.

The quotation marks in the above sentence mean that the group of words they enclose is

_____ (a)   an independent clause

_____ (b)   a paraphrase of Octavia's words

_____ (c)   an exact repetition of Octavia's words

_____ (d)   a parenthetical insertion

— — — — — — — — — — — — — — — —

(c)

6.   What portion of the following sentence should be enclosed in quotation marks?

Octavia told John that she had lost her identification bracelet.

— — — — — — — — — — — — — — — —

None.

7. Because the sentence above contains an *indirect* quotation, it needs no quotation marks. How about this one?

    Octavia told John she had lost her identification bracelet, poor child.

_ _ _ _ _ _ _ _ _ _ _ _ _ _ _ _

Uncertain.

Here, the meaning can be cleared up by the use or non-use of quotation marks. Without them, the sentence above has Octavia being *reported*, not directly *quoted*, and the *writer* is commenting "poor child." But the sentence meaning can be changed by quotation marks, as follows: Octavia told John "She had lost her identification bracelet, poor child." In this case, you are directly reporting Octavia's words, and the comment "poor child" is *by* Octavia, not *about* her.

8. The following sentences have no quotation marks, although some should have. See if you can identify which involve direct and which indirect quotations.

    (a) She said angrily that she'd like to leave.

    (b) So would I he said.

    (c) But her father argued that it was too early.

    (d) But her father argued it's too early.

    (e) He said he would be back soon.

_ _ _ _ _ _ _ _ _ _ _ _ _ _ _ _

(a) indirect; (b) direct; (c) indirect; (d) uncertain (The sentence may be punctuated either: "But," her father argued, "it's too early." or the way it stands. Meaning makes the difference.); (e) indirect

9. The use of quotation marks to indicate the exact words spoken by someone else is sometimes troublesome, especially when the quotation marks must be used with other marks of punctuation. The following examples cover most of these problems. Study them over carefully, then go on to the more detailed explanations which follow.

    (a) He said he would come. (indirect quotation)
    (b) He said, "I will come." (direct quotation)
    (c) He said, "The sky is blue."

(d) He said that the sky is blue.

(e) "The sky," he said, "is blue."

(f) "The sky is blue," he said. "The sun is shining brightly."

(g) He said that the sky is blue and the sun is shining brightly.

(h) "The sky is cloudy today," he said. "Do you think it will rain?"

(i) He asked, "Is the sky blue today?"

(j) Did he say, "The sky is blue"?

(k) Did he ask, "Is the sky blue?"

(l) He spoke of his "old log house"; actually, it was almost a mansion.

(m) He said, "Barnum was right when he said, 'There's a sucker born every minute.' " (*Note: single* quotation marks are used for a quotation within a quotation. [British writers reverse these.])

(n) He asked, "Was Barnum right when he said, 'There's a sucker born every minute'?" (*Note:* In general, when the material being quoted is a question, the question mark falls *inside* the quotation marks. When the material being quoted is not a question, but the rest of the sentence forms a question, the question mark falls *outside* the quotation marks. Here the quotation marks come first, then the question mark which *does* end the whole question, and finally the double quotation marks.)

Punctuate—where necessary—the following:

All hands below! With practiced skill, the lookouts slipped below deck.

Dive! Dive! Dive! the commander shouted, lowering himself through the hatch. Letting the handrails slide through his grasp, he braked his fall and reached up to slam down the hatch-cover.

The Exec was chanting: Pressure in the boat. Green board. Bow planes at 30°. He turned for orders. Speed and depth, Skipper?

All ahead flank. Take her down to 300, responded the commander. He hoped only that the sea would be too murky for the aircraft above to have an easy target. But aloud he said, Right full rudder. Come to 190° true bearing. For encouragement he added, That little corkscrew turn ought to louse up his sightings!

The boat jerked and heaved upward as if a great hand had slapped at her. But the heavy thump of the exploding charge was safely distant, they all knew. Only the commander realized that, but for the lookout's sharpness, that hand might have come much closer.

Relieved, the Exec joked, Did you say, Louse up his sightings, sir? Looks like we really threw him a curve!

Maybe, the commander replied. But in case that guy has another egg to lay, let's give him some problems. Alter course to 210° and come up to 150. With a tight-lipped grin he looked upward. Figure that one out, Flyboy! he growled.

— — — — — — — — — — — — — — — —

"All hands below!" With practiced skill, the lookouts slipped below deck.

"Dive! Dive! Dive!" the commander shouted, lowering himself through the hatch. Letting the handrails slide through his grasp, he braked his fall and reached up to slam down the hatch-cover.

The Exec was chanting: "Pressure in the boat. Green board. Bow planes at 30°." He turned for orders. "Speed and depth, Skipper?"

"All ahead flank. Take her down to 300," responded the commander. He hoped only that the sea would be too murky for the aircraft above to have an easy target. But aloud he said, "Right full rudder. Come to 190° true bearing." For encouragement he added, "That little corkscrew turn ought to louse up his sightings!"

The boat jerked and heaved upward as if a great hand had slapped at her. But the heavy thump of the exploding charge was safely distant, they all knew. Only the commander realized that, but for the lookout's sharpness, that hand might have come much closer.

Relieved, the Exec joked, "Did you say, 'Louse up his sightings,' sir? Looks like we really threw him a curve!"

"Maybe," the commander replied. "But in case that guy has another egg to lay, let's give him some problems. Alter course to 210° and come up to 150." With a tight-lipped grin he looked upward. "Figure that one out, Flyboy!" he growled.

10. As you can see from the above examples, the rule for exclamation points in quotations is the same as that for question marks. Punctuate the following sentences:

Look out she cried.

Boy, you should have heard him do Horatio at the Bridge!

— — — — — — — — — — — — — — — —

"Look out!" she cried.

Boy, you should have heard him do "Horatio at the Bridge"!

11. In the second sentence you have an example of another use for quotation marks: they indicate the title of a piece of writing that is shorter than book length, like a poem, a short story, an essay, or a chapter of a book. Some more examples:

> "I am Born" is the title of the first chapter of Dickens' David Copperfield. (underline books for italic)

> When I was a boy, everyone had to memorize Joyce Kilmer's poem, "Trees." (periods go *inside*)

> Milton's Paradise Lost is an extremely long poem. (Indeed, a book-length work, it is underlined for italic.)

12. Quotation marks are used to show that a word is used in a special way. For example:

> When I say "artificial," I use it here in the sense of made with artifice, or fine craftsmanship.

> Today "romantic" usually means something to do with love.

Note in the first example above that the comma, like the period, goes inside the quotation marks. However semicolons are usually placed outside as they are in sentence (1) in frame 9. You will probably need some practice using quotation marks with other punctuation, but like other punctuation marks they do affect your meaning.

Now, test yourself in using apostrophes and quotation marks by taking the following Self-Test. You can then go on to see how much you've learned from the book by taking the Final Test.

We have covered the basic skills of punctuation, and you should now be able to use these to create your own particular style in writing. Happy writing!

SELF-TEST

This Self-Test will help you determine how well you have met the objectives for this chapter and whether you are ready to go on to the Final Test. The answers to this Self-Test follow.

Rewrite the material in parentheses, using apostrophes where appropriate.

1. The museum walls were lined with the (rifles of the soldiers) captured at Waterloo.

2. The Great Potato Famine of (45) decimated Ireland.

3. (It is) my turn now; (the turn belonging to you) is next.

4. Thirty-three (of the number 3) equal nine (of the number 11).

5. (the plays of Euripides) are more realistic than (those of Sophocles).

6. (the routines belonging to Abbott and Costello) are famous.

7. Their most famous number is "(Who is) on first base?"

8. (this is the hat of who?)

9. (the business of George and Harry) was on the verge of bankruptcy.

10. (the husbands of Mary and Rose) have very different tastes in clothing.

11. (It is) easy to see that (fashions of men) are as much controlled by industry as are (fashions of women).

12. (the cooking of someone else) always tastes better.

13. (the smoke of the tires) blanketed the track.

14. (the jackets of the track workers) were yellow.

Write the possessive form of the following words:

15. man

16. alligator

17. Moses

18. friends

19. anyone

Write the contraction of the following:

20. they are

21. we will

22. ought not

23. might have

24. would not

25. used not

26. we are

Punctuate the following sentences:

27. He said that the sky is blue and the sun is shining brightly.

28. The sky is gray he said, and the sun is hiding behind those clouds.

29. Did he say The sky is blue

30. He asked if it was raining.

31. One of the poems in the book is Lewis Carroll's Jabberwock.

32. That poem added several words to the English language, among them being slithy, mimsy, and borogroves.

33. Drop dead he shouted

34. He asked Did Carroll really originate the word jabberwock

35. Of course he did he answered Why do you doubt it.

36. He wondered why no one else had thought of it.

Answers to Self-Test

Compare your answers to the Self-Test to those given below. If you answered all questions correctly, go on to the Final Test. If you missed any, review the frames indicated in parentheses following the answers. If you missed several questions, you should probably look back over the whole chapter before going on.

1. soldiers' rifles (frame 1)

2. '45 (frame 3)

3.   It's (frame 3), your turn   (frame 4b)

4.   *3*'s; *11*'s   (frame 4)

5.   Euripides' plays; Sophocles'   (frame 1)

6.   Abbott and Costello's routines   (frame 2)

7.   Who's   (frames 3, 4b)

8.   Whose hat is this?   (frame 4b)

9.   George and Harry's business   (frame 2)

10.   Mary's and Rose's husbands   (frame 2)

11.   It's (frame 3); men's fashions (frame 1); women's   (frame 1)

12.   Someone else's cooking   (frame 2)

13.   The tires' smoke   (frame 1)

14.   The track workers' jackets   (frame 1)

15.   man's   (frame 1)

16.   alligator's   (frame 1)

17.   Moses'   (frame 1)

18.   friends'   (frame 1)

19.   anyone's   (frame 1)

20.   they're   (frame 3)

21.   we'll   (frame 3)

22.   oughtn't   (frame 3)

23.   might've   (frame 3)

24.   wouldn't   (frame 3)

25.   usedn't   (frame 3)

26.   we're   (frame 3)

27.   no other punctuation needed   (frames 3, 4d, 4g)

28.   "The sky is gray," he said, "and the sun is hiding behind those clouds."
      (frame 4f)

29.   Did he say, "The sky is blue"?   (frame 4j)

30.   no punctuation needed   (frame 8, 9d, 9g)

31.   One of the poems in the book is Lewis Carroll's "Jabberwock."
      (frame 11)

32. That poem added several words to the English language, among them being "slithy," "mimsy," and "borogroves."   (frame 12)

33. "Drop dead!" he shouted.   (frame 10)

34. He asked, "Did Carroll really originate the word 'jabberwock'?" (frame 9n)

35. "Of course he did," he answered. "Why do you doubt it?"   (frame 9h)

36. no other punctuation needed   (frames 8, 9d, 9g)

Final Test

The following questions are intended to review your overall understanding of the material in this book. The answers to the Final Test follow.

Correcting where necessary, supply punctuation for the following sentences:

1. Its a good thing that you had enough money for both mothers-in-laws corsages

2. The students car wash unfortunately for them had only had three jobs that day a Bentley a Jeep and a Mack truck.

3. Look out she screamed that was a mouse wasnt it

4. Although it seemed unlikely he could pass without studying the student tried anyway

5. Whose fault is that he asked for it was obviously not his

6. Why does he always steal Alices soap flakes when we have a snowstorm to stage

7. Sailing across the Atlantic on the Queen Mary Queen Elizabeth read Gone with the Wind

8. I didnt have enough money to buy another ticket and I had no time to go home for more

9. It was the Japanese not the Germans who precipitated our entry into the war

10. The list read as follows three cans of beans a pound of bacon a loaf of bread two cans of stew a pound of cheese a dozen eggs and a carton of cigarettes

11. John you will notice is embarrassed at being singled out

12. Whose umbrella was left in the mens bar

13. Words meaning the young of a species colts lambs calves etc are usually words having favorable connotations

14. The text for last Sundays sermon was Genesis 28 11

15. Shop Math a Self-Teaching Guide was sold out or he would have bought a copy

16. Before leaving for work he had to clear the driveway of fallen branches carefully avoiding the live power line nearby fill the hole where the roots of the fallen tree had thrown up part of the road-bed clean off the car seat for the windshield had been shattered by a tree-limb and then try to start the water-soaked engine

17. In his Bands of Americans Edgar Glockenspiel writes At the turn of the century lived John Philip Sousa 1854–1932 called the March King p. 95

18. A week later one A.M. he was driving to work along Green St. and saw Harry Smiths Mrs.

19. The statements on the previous three pp have no relationship to the charts on page 368 these charts are also mistakenly reproduced in ch 4

20. Why is it he puzzled that the price of a pound of coffee keeps going down but the price of a cup of coffee keeps going up

21. Speaking on the occasion of the societys third anniversary its founder said this we have seen the great promise of our dreams fulfilled the tree has borne good fruit

22. He said Barnum was right when he said Theres a sucker born every minute

23. George owned several vehicles a Ford truck a snowmobile a moped and a Daimler which kept him constantly broke

24. The prices for the optional equipment were anyone would agree far too high

25. The Electric Boat Co has been the mainstay of our submersible ship-building it has constructed submarines since before the 1st World War

26. The car an old Chevrolet stalled on the hill it was Harry not Jim who got it started

27. I think that car ahead of us is having trouble Jane said look out theyve crashed into the guardrail

28. Although Sousa is given credit some might say blame for the invention of the sousaphone he only suggested its development others designed and built it

29. We read about it in The Forum in The New York Times

30. Thirty five twin screw steel cruisers make too slow moving a fleet certainly to intercept the Russians motor torpedo boats

Answers to the Final Test

Compare your answers with those that follow. If you miss any and wish to go back for review, use the chapter and frame references which follow each answer.

1. It's a good thing that you had enough money for both mothers-in-law's corsages. (chapter 8, frames 3, 2)

2. The students' car wash, unfortunately for them, had only had three jobs that day: a Bentley, a Jeep, and a Mack truck. (chapter 8, frame 1c; chapter 3, frames 5, 3)

3. "Look out!" she screamed. "That was a mouse, wasn't it?" (chapter 8, frames 9h, 10)

4. Although it seemed unlikely he could pass without studying, the student tried anyway. (chapter 3, frame 2)

5. "Whose fault is that?" he asked, for it was obviously not his. (chapter 2, frame 8; chapter 8, frame 9)

6.   Why does he always steal Alice's soap flakes when we have a snowstorm to stage?   (chapter 2, frames 8, 10, 11; chapter 5, frame 1a)

7.   Sailing across the Atlantic on the Queen Mary, Queen Elizabeth read Gone with the Wind.   (chapter 3, frame 2; chapter 6, frames 16, 17)

8.   I didn't have enough money to buy another ticket, and I had no time to go home for more.   (chapter 8, frame 3; chapter 3, frame 1)

9.   It was the Japanese, not the Germans, who precipitated our entry into the war.   (chapter 3, frame 25)

10. The list read as follows: three cans of beans, a pound of bacon, a loaf of bread, two cans of stew, a pound of cheese, a dozen eggs, and a carton of cigarettes.   (chapter 5, frame 1; chapter 3, frames 3, 30)

11. John, you will notice, is embarrassed at being singled out.   (chapter 3, frame 17)

12. Whose umbrella was left in the men's bar?   (chapter 8, frames 4b, 1a; chapter 2, frames 10, 11)

13. Words meaning the young of a species—colts, lambs, calves, etc.—are usually words having favorable connotations.   (chapter 5, frame 12; chapter 3, frames 3, 30; chapter 7, frame 2)

14. The text for last Sunday's sermon was Genesis 28:11.   (chapter 8, frame 1; chapter 5, frame 10)

15. Shop Math: a Self-Teaching Guide was sold out, or he would have bought a copy.   (chapter 6, frame 16; chapter 5, frame 10; chapter 3, frame 1)

16. Before leaving for work he had to: clear the driveway of fallen branches, carefully avoiding the live power-line nearby; fill the hole where the roots of the fallen tree had thrown up part of the road-bed; clean off the car seat, for the windshield had been shattered by a tree-limb; and then try to start the water-soaked engine.   (chapter 5, frame 3; chapter 4, frames 16, 17)

17. In his Bands of Americans Edgar Glockenspiel writes: "At the turn of the century lived John Philip Sousa (1854–1932), called the March King" (p. 95).   (chapter 6, frame 16; chapter 3, frame 2, chapter 6, frame 3; chapter 4, frame 14)

18. A week later, one morning he was driving to work along Green Street and saw Harry Smith's wife [or Mrs. Harry Smith].   (chapter 7, frame 1)

19. The statements on the previous three pages have no relationship to the charts on page 368; these charts are also mistakenly reproduced in Chapter Four.   (chapter 7, frame 5; chapter 4, frames 4, 14)

20. "Why is it," he puzzled, "that the price of a pound of coffee keeps going down, but the price of a cup of coffee keeps going up?" (chapter 4, frames 19, 20; chapter 8, frame 4)

21. Speaking on the occasion of the society's third anniversary, its founder said this: "We have seen the great promise of our dreams fulfilled; the tree has borne good fruit." (chapter 3, frame 2; chapter 5, frame 9; chapter 8, frame 3; chapter 4, frames 14, 15)

22. He said "Barnum was right when he said 'There's a sucker born every minute.' " (chapter 8, frame 9m)

23. George owned several vehicles—a Ford truck, a snowmobile, a moped, and a Daimler—which kept him constantly broke. (chapter 5, frame 12)

24. The prices for the optional equipment were—anyone would agree—far too high. (chapter 5, frames 16–18)

25. The Electric Boat Company has been the mainstay of our submersible ship-building; it has constructed submarines since before the First World War. (chapter 4, frames 5, 14, 15, 19, 20; chapter 7, frame 1)

26. The car, an old Chevrolet, stalled on the hill. It was Harry, not Jim, who got it started. (chapter 3, frames 26, 25; chapter 2, frame 2)

27. "I think that car ahead of us is having trouble," Jane said. "Look out! They've crashed into the guardrail!" (chapter 2, frames 6, 7; chapter 8, frames 9f, 3)

28. Although Sousa is given credit (Some might say blame.) for the invention of the sousaphone, he only suggested its development; others designed and built it. (chapter 6, frame 4; chapter 3, frame 2; chapter 4, frames 5, 6)

29. We read about it in "The Forum" in The New York Times. (chapter 6, frames 16, 17; chapter 8, frame 11)

30. Thirty-five, twin-screw, steel cruisers make too slow-moving a fleet, certainly, to intercept the Russians' motor torpedo boats. (chapter 7, frames 9, 6; chapter 8, frame 1c)

Index